RENEWAL IN WORSHIP

RENEWAL
in
WORSHIP

MICHAEL MARSHALL

MOREHOUSE-BARLOW
Wilton

First published 1982 by Marshall Morgan & Scott,
3 Beggarwood Lane,
Basingstoke, Hants,
RG23 7LP, UK

Revised American edition published 1985 by
Morehouse-Barlow Co., Inc.
78 Danbury Road
Wilton, Connecticut 06897

ISBN 0-8192-1374-8

Library of Congress Catalog Card Number 85-061214

Permission to quote on page 101 from "Sounds of Silence"
by Paul Simon, copyright © 1964 by Paul Simon, is
gratefully acknowledged.

Printed in the United States of America

2 4 6 8 10 9 7 5 3 1

Dedicated to the Reverend Dr. John Andrew in gratitude for his hospitality both in his church—in the pulpit and at the altar—and in his home; and also to the clergy, director of music, choir, and congregation of St. Thomas's Church, Fifth Avenue, New York, where the worship is a converting experience for so many people.

"The Power of God is the worship he inspires."

A.N. Whitehead

Contents

Preface

WRITING A BOOK ABOUT WORSHIP is a perilous undertaking. It depends, of course, to whom it is mainly addressed. If it is to the clergy—the professionals—then the author had better look out! He would be safer to write a book about cooking and dedicate it to the national conference of chefs and catering managements! A better approach might have been to have expressed nothing more than an amateur enthusiasm about worship and to have "offered" the book as little more than another enthusiast's "cookbook," without any of the pretensions either of a gourmet or a chef—and left it there.

But I am deliberately risking more in this book and, in so doing, I am laying myself open to much criticism. For this book is written from a daily concern, which has gone deeper the longer I have been without a church and congregation, and the more my work as a bishop has taken me round many churches both in the British Isles, the United States of America, and throughout the worldwide Anglican communion. Worship is the gospel in action. There are signs today that people are returning to Christian life and commitment. What will they find in the principal activity of the Church's life? My fear is that they might find the worship of the Church today the biggest stumbling block to living faith.

All kinds of reasons have contributed to bringing about this situation. The liturgical revolution of the second half of the century is still with us and few clergy or laity have yet found their feet

in this lengthy and disturbing process. Then there is the fact that
many clergy who are in responsible positions in the church today
have lived through a time when worship ranked rather low on the
agenda of the Church. There was the fear and unquestioned as-
sumption, in the fifties and sixties, that to be concerned with
the details of worship was to turn your back on the more serious
and compelling issues of the world and contemporary society:
concern about worship was either for the liturgical scholar or
the churchy Christian; the real and rugged apostolate had more
pressing concerns.

This means that in so many churches today, the faithful are
seriously underfed: there is a problem of malnutrition at the heart
of the Christian Church. So this book is written with a note of
urgency, the sort of urgency that is inevitable when hunger and
famine are in the air. It is a challenge, first to the professionals,
the ministers of religion, and all who have been especially charged
with the ministry of word and sacrament. (In addition to the clergy
I would like also to address this book to all seminarians, and even
hope that this particular essay will become a "must" on the reading
list of all who are training as ministers of word, preaching, and
sacrament.) If this is your calling, nothing can be spared in making
certain that for those who already come to church a banquet of
word and worship is being prepared for next Sunday or whenever
and wherever God's people are next to meet for worship. That
will require skill and commitment to this specific ministry within
the whole body of the Church as well as the continual gifts of God's
grace. Properly undertaken, it will in its turn renew and equip God's
people for all the other ministries and tasks that rightly have a place
on the agenda of the church today. But first things first: get this
right and all else will follow. The renewal of the churches today
converges *inwards* on worship, preaching, and commitment and
then explodes *outwards* in evangelism, service, and concern for
the world.

I have a particular wish that this book will transcend the barriers
of churchmanship and the labels of parties within the Church. I
was delighted to receive the invitation to write this book from John

Hunt of Marshall, Morgan and Scott after a lecture I gave in Dublin in 1980 at a renewal conference with Michael and Jeanne Harper. I am even more delighted that since I have come to settle in the United States, Morehouse-Barlow has seen fit to publish a revised edition of the original work. I am especially grateful to Steve Wilburn for his interest in my written works and for his constructive and helpful suggestions about revising this particular book for publication in America. Although I must accept total responsibility for the views expressed in these pages, I would nevertheless like to think that much of what is written here is in the spirit of that most blessed movement of renewal sweeping through all the churches at the present time.

But there is more to this book than the energies of a one-man band. I am very grateful to Miss Ferrar, the editor of *Search*—the journal of the Church of Ireland—who reproduced my original lectures mentioned above, from very scrappy notes, in that excellent quarterly. Mary Baddeley, without whom no book of mine would ever have been completed, gave unstintingly of her time and enthusiasm in typing the manuscript as well as in goading the reluctant author to complete his task. Some friends and clergy from the diocese of Southwark who shared my enthusiasm about the priority of well-ordered worship arranged workshops on various occasions during which some of the content of these pages was tested and tried out. Revising and extending the original book proved a more exacting task than I had first envisaged, and I would wish to record my grateful appreciation to The Reverend Charles Bewick, my chaplain and colleague in the Gospel for his considerable and inspiring help in this task. I also extend my appreciation to Ann Scott and Sally and Bob Barrett who carefully and under pressure of time corrected the proofs of the "Revised Standard Edition" of yet another one of my books.

RENEWAL IN WORSHIP

Worship and the Human Condition

W HY WAS I CREATED?" is the fundamental question posed in the Scottish Catechism. "I was created in order to worship God and to enjoy him forever." If that reply is true, then it strikes at the whole basis of the human condition. Every man, woman, and child was created for worship. The statement is universal in its application and is not restricted simply to people who go to church or who happen to like that sort of thing. Worship is the basic, fundamental instinct within every creature, an instinct more basic and more lasting than our sexual instincts and yet an instinct scarcely heeded in the ordinary daily conversation and concerns of twentieth-century man—to say nothing of its blatant neglect in the syllabus of contemporary education.

"If you don't worship you'll shrink: it's as brutal as that," explodes the psychiatrist in the play *Equus*.[1] In other words, like all basic instincts, if it is neglected it does not evaporate or just go away; it wounds, perverts, and corrupts, because man, if he is made for worship, will demand expression in one way or another of that compulsive drive. From our early childhood, we have experienced the strange power and release of worship in one form or another. For so fundamental is the experience of, and instinct for, worship, that it pre-dates verbal expression and transcends even the most sophisticated vocabulary. Hence, children and illiterate people are not excluded from its power or its claims. Indeed, we can go further

1

and say that for those who have not yet reached the age when they are restricted by the inhibition of words, the doors to worship are more easily opened and the checks and brakes of rationalism are not so easily applied. The power of the numinous is more in evidence when reason is least aggressive and herein lie both the potential and also the dangers of worship.

For, by definition, worship must be that moment when we no longer retain the initiative. The word numinous indicates a moment or a place when the world around me *beckons* me. I no longer stick to the facts; rather, a strange and even bewildering experience begins when it would seem as though the reality is the other way round; the facts seem to stick to me! We can never be totally safe from the invasion of such a moment, for it necessarily takes us unawares. It can be that moment when the sun is setting or the moon is rising. It can be the occasion of a familiar and frequently heard piece of music, a work of art, or the presence of a person. Such numinous moments begin to draw me and take me out of myself. For a moment, I am lost.

> And man, the marvel seeing,
> Forgets his selfish being
> For joy of beauty not his own.[2]

"Lost in wonder, love and praise"[3]—a moment or a place of worship demands that we transcend ourselves. Such moments and places can belong to a whole discipline—like art, music or poetry —that is deliberately calculated to evoke adoration. But a "perfectly ordinary" place or a "perfectly ordinary person," a common, everyday sound or a sight can suddenly be endowed with a *significance* and a complex may be formed that probably will not disappear for the rest of our lives. Suddenly it is not so much that I see a different world, but rather that I see the same world very differently. A whole new perspective opens out in front of me. We frequently speak of such moments as moments of inspiration, when we catch our breath. These are times of illumination, which tempt us to suppose that we must have been blind before: "There it was, staring me in the face and I couldn't see it." "My God, now

I see!" Sometimes the result brings great joy, great sorrow, or a sense of deep disintegration. What is quite clear is that we can never go back again to seeing things as we used to see them. We are initiated into a totally new perspective, with a new outlook as a result of this devastating new insight. The New Testament word for this is *metanoia*—generally translated by the ecclesiastical word "repentance," but perhaps more accurately understood as a change of outlook because of a new insight. In fact, worship and repentance at their best belong together, as we shall see later in our discussion. Where worship does not issue in repentance, there is a strong probability that all kinds of complexes, "hang-ups," and difficulties will arise. For it is the strange ability of a scene or a smell or even architecture to take to itself something special that sets it aside, rendering it in some sense holy and different. We are suddenly aware, as surely as Jacob in the Old Testament, that we are on holy ground; instincts are aroused that our cautious intellect may have told us were safely hidden beneath the veneer of sophistication and rationalization.

The power of worship can bind together in a totally irrational way a particular substance with a particular sensation, a particular time with a particular impression, a particular place with a never-to-be forgotten experience. We can become prisoners, even fetishists, through this experience of worship, through this bondage of association. Not all worship sets us free, and we need to be reminded frequently that even the devil has his contemplatives. We can flee to the darkness and be imprisoned by it, just as surely as insects are fatally drawn to the light and consumed by it. We need the discipline of repentance to realign the world of our experience so that the experience and the context find their true perspective in our world view.

For not all worship is good or true; we need to *learn* to worship as surely as we have to learn to do properly what at first came to us by instinct. What a child at first does by nature has to be relearned if it is to "stand up" in the adult world. The instinct to worship, as surely as any other instinct in our lives, needs to be directed if it is not to become corrupted. Every political tyrant since the dawn of history has known the power of worship and the compulsive need within every human being to express this instinct and to find objects for that worship. When the instinct to worship is wrongly directed, there are scarcely any limits to the depravity to which the human race can sink. From the crimes of Nazism to the mass suicide of the People's Temple in Guyana in 1979, we can see the power and the persuasiveness of worship when it has gone wrong and when it has been perverted.

> A man may divert his powers of worship away from God and set it upon himself or even upon the State. For people who know nothing about the true God, or who, though knowing God, are not interested in him, may still worship. For the fact that such worship is not directed to its true end does not prevent it being real worship. But worship of what is less than God, or opposed to God, though real, is harmful. Therefore it is essential that man shall learn to worship the true god and to give his homage where it rightly belongs. For to worship is to acknowledge with every part of one's being the worth-ship of what is worshipped, to acknowledge with the mind, the affections and the will its utter perfection. To commit oneself *thus* towards what is imperfect or perishable is to engender the lie in the soul: while *thus* to render homage to what objectively claims it, namely Almighty God, is to take one's appointed place in the universe and to do what each of us was born to do.[4]

Precisely because it is so powerful and so able to transcend the rationalizing processes, embracing the whole personality in every way, worship needs to be disciplined and sanctified if it is not to destroy its practitioners.

Throughout the whole of the Old Testament the great caution is against idolatry. There is always the temptation to worship false gods. If the true God is not available to worship (as was the case with Aaron and the children of Israel at the foot of Mount Sinai), then mankind will fashion gods of their own making. The golden calf is never very far away and is always ready to masquerade as an alternative possibility for compulsive worshippers. The home-spun gods of Isaiah, taking different forms in different ages, are always turning their worshippers into slaves and condemning them to life-long bondage.[5] The tin gods of our own making are easily recognizable, for they always enslave those who worship them. It is the distinctive mark of the worship of the one true and living God that he is the only God who risks giving back to his worshippers an ever increasing freedom. All other gods are the gods of the Egyptians and belong to our immaturity and the chapters of bondage in our lives. It is only the living God who repeats again and again: "Let my people go."[6]

So, then, Jesus demands in the New Testament that our worship shall be "in spirit and in truth."[7] We must learn to transfer all our instincts for worship to the one true and living God: "To love him in all things and above all things."[8] In true worship we lose ourselves—our old selves—but in turn, the living God gives us back our true and new selves. "For freedom has Christ set us free."[9] Every other liberator so often leaves us "hung up," as we say, on the very objects of our worship. An age hungry for kicks will always be dangerously open to the call to let go and let God! But this hysterical and enthusiastic statement presupposes the very question with which the Bible is rightly concerned from cover to cover, namely, which God? "Let go" may well be very important in an age indoctrinated for too long by the tyranny of the intellect, but it is far more important to question into what we are letting go. Of course worship brings release and people who have been starved of the opportunity to worship or strongly cautioned to be suspicious of the inexplicable will soon begin to search for such a release. "Let go," however, could presumably have been the call to the gadarene swine as they chorused together "and so say all of us," heading disastrously towards the precipice! For there will always be great dangers in a quest that demands an unquestioning attitude. The unquestioning compulsive worshipper *knows* he is right; he is on the "right wavelength" and that is a very dangerous place to be!

It was Teilhard de Chardin who said that in the end there were only two alternatives for mankind: adoration or annihilation. It is a strong statement but it is profoundly true. Adoration is the superlative of love, yet love frustrated is never very far from hatred.

The Church's responsibility to teach men and women to worship the true and living God is an awesome and terrifying responsibility.

There was a time when religion and learning were joined together. At such a time discernment was set within worship. Worshippers met in buildings where architecture and design invited the healthy experience of the transcendent. In such environments heart and mind could grow together. Worship was informed by truth and moral commitment; scholarship was lifted beyond itself in the fuller environment of adoration. In many schools and universities in many parts of the so-called Christian world, however, worship has no place whatever in the timetable. Religion, insofar as it is taught, is the poor relation of all the other disciplines in the curriculum and lingers a long way behind them as just another subject imparted only through the mind and the intellect. Modern man is wildly open, therefore, to every false god and the claims that false gods make and so he is easily duped once he enters the sanctuary of worship where he is not at home and for which he has not been trained. His experience of the numinous and the inevitable quest for the transcendent easily deteriorate into a dangerous and morbid curiosity. It is precisely this that feeds the ever increasing market at the present time for white and black magic. The cult of the occult is not going to disappear in an age that is hungry for kicks and that needs to break loose from the prison of the intellect. Witches' covens have not disappeared with the Middle Ages. They are back with us again, populated so often by the sophisticated and those who have the spiritual age and discernment of a few-weeks'-old baby. Dissociation between religion and learning may well be answerable for many of the ills of our present time.

Therefore, ministers of religion need to be recalled to their primary task of ministering to the religious needs of people and the worshipping instinct within mankind. Such ministry is a skill. It has to be learned. Lost in a labyrinth of false alternatives, mankind must be shown a route to the truth and the warmth of the sunshine. The route is hazardous, precisely because it is best found in those very areas of human experience most often neglected or, worse still, just abandoned to an uncharted instinct, uninformed by reason or truth. The call to the Christian minister of religion is to school others in a worship that is both "spirit-filled" and a revelation of the truth. It is that elusive and yet vastly important enterprise that is the activity and responsibility of the Church in its daily life and in its services of public worship week by week. When worship really comes alive it is a very intoxicating and a very dangerous and powerful experience. It is not an accident that at the first Pentecost the spirit-filled apostles were mistakenly regarded by many as drunk.[10] In all ecstatic experiences, and whenever and wherever men and women are released through the transcendence of worship, there is always the possibility of confusing and overlapping phenomena. This is hardly surprising. For a finite creature to experience and to "take on" something of what by definition is infinite is not unlike trying to transcribe an orchestral symphony for piano or to reproduce a three-dimensional scene on a two-dimensional piece of paper. In the former case one note on the piano would have to represent several sounds (flute, oboes, and strings); in the latter case a diagonal line would sometimes signify a diagonal line and sometimes a line in depth that can be reproduced in no other way. So with many intensely deep and even dramatic reponses to worship. Laughing, crying, tongues, can all be explained in a reductionist way as "merely" laughing (irreverence), or merely hysteria (tears or tongues). Indeed, that may be the explanation. Nevertheless, the same expression may be better explained in a totally different way. A fit of the giggles (like Sarah in the Old Testament), or baptism with tears, or release in tongues are well attested religious phenomena and can occur whenever finite men and women are faced with the transcendent and the infinite. Discernment, therefore, is required if we are to distinguish between two very different causes in diagnosing the same symptom. It is not by chance that we seem to have toppled at this point into medical language. A minister of religion must be also a physician of the soul, able to exercise discernment wherever renewal is occurring and not least in places where the power of worship is released.

For too long many churches in the west, and especially the reformed churches, have placed worship low on the list of priorities. At best it has become a means to an end. It has been there to edify, to exhort, and to aid the good life. It was William Temple who used to say that most people thought that the end of human life was the good life, with worship as the means to that end. In fact, as he so rightly commented, the reverse is the truth: the end of man is to worship and the good life is one of the means to that end. "People are always thinking that conduct is supremely important, and that because prayer helps it, therefore prayer is good. That is true as far as it goes: still truer is it to say that worship is of supreme importance and conduct tests it."[11] If the quotation with which our chapter began is true, then it will be worship that continues when all else has ceased. "After this I looked, and behold, a great multitude which no man could number, from every nation, from all tribes and peoples and tongues, standing before the throne and before the Lamb. . . . [T]hey fell on their faces before the throne and worshipped God."[12] The Bible begins with creation and ends with worship. That is the direction in which we must all move. The social gospel, commitment to the concerns of the Third World, care for the environment, the right ordering of our resources—all these are important concerns for the churches at the present time, but they will only find their true perspective in the total picture of Christian discipleship if they flow from and are transcended by the true purpose and goal of all creation—worship and adoration. The purpose and peace of mankind is only to be found ultimately in the worship of the One who created us.

> Untune that string,
> And, hark! what discord follows.[13]

So from the outset let us be under no illusion about the importance of our subject. Worship is vital; worship is crucial to man's survival and sanity; worship is powerful and dangerous, demanding direction; it is most certainly "not a rule of safety—it is an adventure of the spirit." Those words from a larger statement by Whitehead leave no doubt about the importance that great

Cambridge mathematician and philosopher attached to worship. He wrote:

> Religion is the vision of something which stands beyond, behind, and within, the passing flux of immediate things; something which is real, and yet waiting to be realized; something which is a remote possibility, and yet the greatest of present facts; something that gives meaning to all that passes, and yet eludes apprehension; something whose possession is the final good, and yet is beyond all reach. . . . The immediate reaction of human nature to the religious vision is worship. . .and worship is a surrender to the claim for assimilation, urged with the motive force of mutual love. The vision never over-rules. It is always there, and it has the power of love presenting the one purpose whose fulfilment is eternal harmony. The power of God is the worship he inspires. That religion is strong which in its ritual and its modes of thought evokes an apprehension of the commanding vision. The worship of God is not a rule of safety—it is an adventure of the spirit, a flight after the unattainable. The death of religion comes with the repression of the high hope of adventure.[14]

The Nature and Characteristics of Christian Worship

We have seen how worship is the universal instinct rooted deeply within mankind and that it is therefore neither restricted to the activity of a particular religion, nor is it only to be found in buildings specifically set aside for it. Worship is at the heart of all world religions, and it is true to say that religion focuses and harnesses this instinct that is so powerfully latent in all human beings, whether they would care to call themselves religious or not. Christian teaching about worship, however, goes further and says that when all else has ceased, it will be worship that remains as the very nature of our relationship as creatures to our creator. The last word of the Bible in the book of Revelation gives us a picture of worship, but so also does the first word in the opening chapter of Genesis. In Genesis we see a picture of God enjoying and delighting in what he has made—his creation. In Revelation we catch a glimpse of man enjoying and delighting in the One who made him—his creator. If it is right to say that "we love because he first loved us,"[1] might it not also be true to say that we delight in God, adore and worship him, because he first delighted in us? And worshipped us? Dare we say that?

Yes, in some sense we dare, because worship means also "worthship" and in those opening chapters of Genesis we see God endowing his creation with its true worth. Mankind, in comparison with the rest of creation, has little value, significance, or worth:

compared with the hills and the mountains we are transient, here today and gone tomorrow; compared with the sea and other natural elements we are weak and ineffective. It is only in our relationship with God—our capacity to know him, worship, love, and adore him—that mankind finds its significance and worth. So our lasting value as human beings can only truly be derived from the one who created us. The flaw, however, is that we lost our hearts to the wrong things, creating a topsy-turvy world of false values with false gods. These false gods rapidly became rival gods with price tags around their necks out of all proportion to their real and lasting value. It may not be stretching a point too far to say that an age of economic chaos is no accident, for if we do not know where we are going we can hardly be expected to know what is a fair price for the journey! We are unable to identify objects worthy of our worship, as God, in his turn, is no longer able to recognize the work of his hand and his image in his creation. It is only in Jesus Christ that God once again comes to take delight in his creation, and both at the baptism and at the transfiguration of Jesus, the cry of *deja vu* is repeated: "You are my well beloved Son in whom once again I come to take delight."[2] The way of worship is once again now from both ends: the Son glorifies the Father, the Father glorifies the Son, and those who are in the Son become once again acceptable and recognizable by the Father and the God who created them.

So we can see how the Bible, from cover to cover, is the story of worship and how God's people in the Old and New Testaments alike are a worshipping people. We shall not be surprised to find at the outset many crude expressions of worship with all the dangers that attain to such immature insights. Nevertheless, slowly that worship is purified, not developing in a straightforward way or progressing smoothly, but rather lurching unsteadily—now going back again to earlier patterns, and now reaching forward to refined and more God-centered worship—until at last it is perfected in the one who is himself alone and only the one true perfect, sufficient sacrifice, offering and oblation, acceptable to God—Jesus Christ our Lord and Savior. In Jesus, all the ingredients of inadequate and unacceptable worship are focused, redeemed and redirected to create "a sweet smelling savour"[3] acceptable to God.

So we need, however briefly and inadequately, to trace the course of the history of worship in the Bible. We will see how it has evolved with all the elements common to all forms of worship and yet at the same time with the distinctive features of biblical worship belonging peculiarly to the redemption and reorientation of worship in Christ. In the Old Testament we read of sacred places, sacred objects, and sacred persons, the sanctuary, the ark, altars, priests, sacred times (feasts and the sabbath), and general acts of worship such as purifications, consecrations, sacrifices, prayer in all its forms, fasting, and prohibitions. These are the ingredients common to worship in all major religions. In earlier times, much of this worship expresses itself in little more than pantheism and animism. The creator and the creation are inseparable and confused; and therefore fertility gods, the gods of the harvest and the fruits of the earth, are worshipped. The great showdown between Jehovah and Baal-worship in the time of Elijah is no isolated occasion,[4] for the Bible is the story of a long process during which the God of history is unravelled from the gods of nature and true worship from the characteristics of worship that belonged to other peoples and tribes with whom God's people were daily involved. Essentially, the God of the Old Testament distinguishes himself from other gods by his historical activity, his saving deeds, and his mighty acts. William Temple writes:

> On the biblical view the locus, the sphere, the area of revelation, is primarily the historic event, not thoughts in men's minds at all, but the thing that happens—the deliverance from Egypt, the retreat of Sennacherib, the exile, and the return. In these things we are to read the action of God, his purpose, his judgement.[5]

God, in the Old Testament, is not the invention of men's minds, born from reflection and speculation, but rather he is the God of revelation, delighting to reveal himself in hard-edged historical events in which he shows his hand, his purpose, and something of his person. The challenge put by Elijah to the gods of Baal is that they also should show their hand in an event of incontrovertible disclosure. Only by such an act can the true God distinguish himself from the false gods who have neither hands nor noses, who smell not, who walk not and who even have to be carried about![6] It is this God, the true and living God who alone is faithful to his people through these mighty acts: a people who in their turn must be faithful to God in giving to him—and to him alone—their worship, adoration, and commitment.

So it is a long—and sometimes tedious—story, in which the people of the Old Israel learn that not everything that passes for worship is acceptable to God—the true and living God. Also that creation does not in fact reflect truthfully the person and features of its creator, but rather must be distinguished from the creator. C.S. Lewis speaks of this, for it is not just an ancient problem, but rather it is a recurring and ever-present deception. We are always to some extent in danger of mistaking the creature for the creator, and we are always ready to turn the icon of creation in all its forms into an idol to which we will give our worship. "These things," writes Lewis, "if they are mistaken for the thing itself, turn into dumb idols, breaking the hearts of their worshippers. For they are not the thing itself; they are only the scent of a flower we have not found, the echo of a tune we have not heard, news from a country we have never yet visited."[7] The creation, even at its best, offers only ambivalent evidence about the nature of the God who created it; mankind's own contribution in God's continuing creative activity persistently distorts his handiwork so that the creation presents a flawed and therefore unreliable image, deceiving those who are tempted to use it as a vehicle for worshipping its creator. The existence of God, beyond and apart from his creation, demands a worship that does not confuse him with his creation, so that pantheism, animism, and idolatry must first be teased out of all worship if such worship is to be acceptable to God—worship "in spirit and in truth." Idolatry is never far below the surface wherever the instinct for worship is at its strongest: in art, music, poetry, in "high church" and beautiful ceremonial. The challenge at the end of the contest between Jehovah and Baal is still the challenge that we need to hear wherever we are drawn most strongly to worship: "How long will you go limping with two different opinions? If the Lord is God, follow him; but if Baal, then follow him."[8]

The confusion between the creator and his creation is, however, but one of many hazards facing worshippers. For holy places have the continuing and perverse habit of becoming high places with their own cults. The local shrine and local cultic worship with their associations of human sacrifice and ritual prostitution appear frequently in the Old Testament. The story of Jacob's ladder is of course one of the many memorable stories—memorable because it rings many bells with our own religious experience. Jacob sets up an altar after his dream and vision and names the place with a special name.[9] How very true that is for all worshippers, for we all have our places that are sacred alone to us, where we have experienced the presence of God in some, possibly spectacular, way. We may well even have our own "nicknames" for them or return to them in pilgrimage whenever we need to recall with thankfulness all that God has done for us and all that he has given to us. Nevertheless, the Old Testament contains a strong warning against such powerful experiences and certainly against ecstasy with the dangerous desire to repeat such experiences. If we do so, we fall prey to the dark side of our religion or even to the occult, which is never far away whenever religious experience is at its strongest. Old Testament customs that may, in our more sophisticated age, seem barbaric and totally alien, can still play tricks with us. For sophistication is always a "pushover" for superstition and we need to remember that human sacrifice, ritual prostitution, and the occult are present in any age—including our own—and do not automatically disappear in the name of progress. The religious seeker in every age must be reminded that Jacob's vision was a given moment from a giving and gracious God. Such moments of ecstasy and spiritual awareness in worship are gifts. Gifts are made to be received and not achieved, received but not repeated nor manipulated nor contrived for their own sake or for the sake of "kicks" associated with them.

From early and primitive forms of folk religion the distinctive elements of Hebrew worship slowly emerged. The focus of this worship was at first the ark as the symbol of God's presence among his people. It was a sign of God's redemptive acts in delivering the chosen people from their enemies. At first movable, the ark rested in various sanctuaries (for example at Shiloh), and for a pilgrim people without stable geographical territory this was a living and sacramental sign of God's love and presence in their midst.

The story of David's and Solomon's desire to build a substantial temple as a "resting place" for God is a telling and lovely account of religious experience and religious desire, but it shows us many of the pitfalls associated with them. The temple was to be the only place for sacrificial worship (viz., Deuteronomy 12) and this is clearly a strong counterattack upon localized high places, shrines, and altars. Of course we can see how localized sacrifice at local shrines was always in danger of becoming so indigenous that it merely reflected the local folk religion and before long became syncretistic and indistinguishable from the pagan worship of the area. We can see, on the other hand, how the establishment of a kingdom under David and the territorial settlement of David's victories gave to God's wandering people a sense of national identity —a king, a capital, and therefore a temple—rather than an identity based on God alone. Nevertheless, all worship and the life of the church needs to have about it this tension between what is local and therefore close to degenerating into folk religion on the one hand, and what is catholic, universal, and distinctive to Christian worship on the other hand. Our worship must be both local and universal. It must certainly reflect what is local and belongs to the community. So often Christian missionaries have made the mistake of trying to export the gospel wrapped up in language, music, and an approach utterly alien to the culture of the missionary field. We need to meet folk religion and embrace it before we can redirect it. In our own day in many areas of the inner city a sophisticated middle class with a largely cerebral religion has failed to incarnate faith and worship in the culture of the local community, with devastating results. A really incarnational religion for a pilgrim people will wish to reaffirm what is local, passing, and even temporary in language, music, and style, for only in this way will it be free from the equal dangers of the cultic, centralized, and formalized worship of "the temple." Nevertheless, if the life and worship of the church are only local and contemporary, then they reflect only half the story. Worship must have about it the wider claims of what is universal "for all men at all times"—what is truly catholic. Local and universal, contemporary and ageless: these should form two sides of the same coin in a worship that is of the spirit and committed to truth. This relationship between what is changeable and what is changeless will perhaps most conspicuously cause tension in the most sensitive area of the practice of worship.

In all the Old Testament discussions about worship, perhaps the strongest note of caution and the most earnest plea to seek redirection came from the prophets. They proclaimed that loyalty to Israel's God, linked with obedience to his will, is the overriding condition for authentic worship. The saving God of the Exodus and the Decalogue is a holy God who demands that the people whom he would mold into a priestly nation shall also be holy: "Say to the congregation of the people of Israel, You shall be holy; for I the Lord your God am holy."[10]

Worship is no substitute for obedience and morality and that is the note struck from the earliest times in the words of Samuel the prophet:

> Has the Lord as great delight in burnt offerings and sacrifices, as in obeying the voice of the Lord? Behold, to obey is better than sacrifice, and to harken than the fat of rams. For rebellion is as the sin of divination, and stubbornness is an iniquity and idolatry.[11]

This must surely be a recurring reminder in every age to would-be worshippers. Worship and service belong together and both are directed first and foremost to God in a life of discipleship. This theme is continuous throughout the Old Testament. The later prophets of the eighth century are so adamant about the priority of obedience that we could sometimes be forgiven for supposing that they really do not see much place for worship at all. That of course is not so. They base their prophecy on the presupposition that worship is the basis of all religious observance. Nevertheless, they do wish to emphasize that such worship needs to issue in obedience if it is to be authentic. So Amos pronounces without equivocation:

> I hate, I despise your feasts [says the Lord], and I take no delight in your solemn assemblies. Even though you offer me your burnt offerings and cereal offerings, I will not accept them, and the peace offerings of your fatted beasts I will not look upon. Take away from me the noise of your songs; to the melody of your harps I will not listen. But let justice roll down like waters, and righteousness like an ever-flowing stream.[12]

So again with Isaiah:

> When you come to appear before me, who requires of you this trampling of my courts? Bring no more vain oblations; incense is an abomination to me. New moon and sabbath and the calling of assemblies—I cannot endure iniquity and solemn assembly. Your new moons and your appointed feasts my soul hates; they have become a burden to me, I am weary of bearing them. When you spread forth your hands, I will hide my eyes from you; even though you make your many prayers, I will not listen; your hands are full of blood. Wash yourselves; make yourselves clean; remove the evil of your doings from before my eyes; cease to do evil, learn to do good; seek justice, correct oppression; defend the fatherless, plead for the widow.[13]

Ben Sira in the book of Ecclesiasticus is just as insistent when he writes: "The Most High is not pleased with the offerings of the ungodly; and he is not propitiated for sins by a multitude of sacrifices."[14] And again: "The offering of a righteous man anoints the altar and its pleasing odor rises before the Most High."[15]

So this relationship of works to worship is a constant theme of renewal in worship in the Old Testament. Throughout religious history there has always been a tension between the cult of the temple and the call of the prophets. The cult, without prophecy and the word, rapidly degenerates into mere ceremonial obsession, with every detail of sanctuary drill as the only priority. Equally, prophecy and the word without worship and sacraments is in serious danger of becoming merely cerebral and moralistic. Each needs the other and each is' fulfilled and expressed in the other. The reaction against a cultic and degenerate catholicism in the Middle Ages was the moralistic, wordy, and cerebral religion of the Reformation. Happily, renewal in the Church today has brought prophecy and the cult of the temple together. As we see in chapter eight, renewal demands that a renewed life be fed and sustained in worship and sacrament and that worship, in its turn, witnesses to concern for the slum, the poor, and those in need. The history of the Old Testament is a long tug-of-war between the two in which in the end both lost! For it is only in the life and witness of Jesus that both worship and obedience come together and are acceptable to the Father.

Perhaps the place in the Old Testament where we see the richest and fullest agenda of all the implications of worship is in the well-known passage of Isaiah (the sixth chapter) in the story of the prophet's vision. It begins, as all worship must, when the prophet enters into a realization of the presence, the holiness, and the glory of God. That moment is the given moment of the numinous with all the power that is latent within such religious experience. It is a moment of vision and insight. It is a moment when the doors of perception, normally closed by man's cerebral censorship, are flung wide open. Ears, which had previously seemed deaf, begin at last to hear. Eyes, which must have been blind in the past, are opened at last. It is a definite moment in time (the year of King Uzziah's death), yet its significance breaks through the limits of time and the finite into the realms of eternity and the infinite. It is localized in the temple, yet its message not only strikes at the heart of the nation but also has spoken most eloquently to men and women of every age and every culture. The vision speaks at the same time of the glory of God and the holiness of God. Here is no religious "kick" for its own sake but rather a demanding clarion call originating in eternity yet speaking directly to men and women in history, calling the nation to repentance and its citizens to service within the community. The impact, reverberating with glory from the heart of heaven, powerfully evokes a sense of sin. Worship and a sense of unworthiness come in the same breath. They invite repentance, renewal, and rededication. The ecstatic had brought about a dislodging of perspective for Isaiah as real as the physical dislodging suffered by Jacob when he was lamed in his wrestle with God. The prophet finds himself seeing things now from a very different viewpoint, and a very uncomfortable viewpoint at that. There can be nothing cheap about such a gracious and given moment; it will issue in nothing less than costly commitment to the voice and purposes of God—a renewal of life and a new obedience in service.

So, those eight verses of Isaiah spell out all that is meant by true worship to a true and living God: vision, repentance, service, and ministry. Yet such an answer begs all the questions. As the Old Testament grew increasingly conscious of the scope of true worship, so it began increasingly to realize that man is in the end incapable of such an offering. The height of his religious consciousness was also the moment of his greater religious torment. Such is the dilemma of the Old Testament writers. At the highest point of their insight into the nature of true worship, they discovered man to be impotent and incapable. This is set out perhaps at its most poetic by the psalmist.

> Sacrifice, and meat-offering, thou wouldst not: but mine eyes hast thou opened
> Burnt-offerings, and sacrifice for sin, hast thou not required: then said I, Lo I come,
> In the volume of the book it is written of me, that I should fulfill thy will, O my God: I am content to do it; yea, thy law is within my heart.[16]

Here is the religious consciousness of the Old Testament, its understanding at last opened fully by God, reaching out to the One who was to come who would do precisely what true worship demanded. In his heart would be the law of God and in his life and vocation God's will for mankind would be fulfilled even to the point of "sacrifice for sin." In him, and in him alone, worship would achieve

its integrity. Christians recognize in Jesus Christ the answer to the
questions posed in the Old Testament about authentic worship
and see all their worship and oblation in the one great perfect
offering of Christ in his incarnation, passion, death, resurrection,
ascension, and glorification. This unrepeatable and sufficient activity
is continually recalled and filled with the prayer, worship, and
intercession of the Church in every age.[17] Christ is our worship.
Wherever this one great offering of Christ is remembered by his
people there is the "temple," whether it be in a small village church,
at a house communion for an old and housebound lady with two
or three neighbors, or at a glorious act of worship in some vast
and beautiful cathedral. Jesus Christ is the size and shape of Christian
worship, drawing together all the conflicting strands of insight from
Old Testament worship, refining (though never emasculating or
falsely spiritualizing) even the earliest and most primitive urges
for worship known in the Old Testament world and to all other
world religions.

Since this is so, Christian worship belongs within the strong
framework of Christian spirituality and Christian doctrine. It should
not be inhibited by either spirituality or doctrine, but it always needs
to be informed by them. With so many changes in the ordering
of worship throughout all the churches in recent years, many
people—not only the faithful laity—find themselves confused,
irritated, and distracted by what can so often appear to be either
change for change's sake or just the vicar's latest fad and whim:
"He likes doing it this way!" But, if worship is to play a proper
place in the renewal of the Church, it must be seen as the outward
and visible sign of our spirituality and our belief about God, Christ,
and his Church. In other words, renewal in worship is only the
tip of the iceberg; it requires a secure and massive undergirding
with teaching, teaching, and more teaching. If Jesus Christ is "the
shape and size of Christian worship," then what we do when we
come together as the Body of Christ should have about it the
features of Christ and what we know of him in his saving work.
The doctrine of his incarnation and baptism as well as of his passion,
death, and resurrection should all take to themselves the flesh and

blood of worship, not only expounded through the words of scripture but acted out in the shape of the liturgy and made explicit in the contours of our prayer. The worship of the Orthodox Churches of the east at first always appears complicated to western Christians. If, however, we see it for what it is—a sacrament of God's activity in creation and redemption—then we may see that it makes apparent in the most effective way possible a living doctrine and a broad and vast spirituality. Although it must not set out simply and only to be didactic, worship must nevertheless relate always to what is taught and believed.

Pope Paul VI wrote in October 1957:

> To link the sacred and the secular
> in such rapport
> that the first
> and the second
> is not altered but sanctified:
> this is the mystery
> of the Incarnation of God made Man
> which liturgy prolongs.

You could scarcely find a better summary of true Christian worship. Precisely because the word of God has enfleshed himself in all that is human and of this world, by and through worship all that is of this world can be redirected and reformed (without being deformed or contaminated) and be lifted to the presence of the holy. The hinge on which all this turns is Christ and all who are in him. Just as the psalmist of old delighted to recall the mighty acts of God in the history of Israel and see this as the central activity of praise and worship,[18] so the Christian of the new Israel delights to recall and reenact the saving acts of God in Christ.

But there must be a real sense of rapport between the sacred and secular. We can have a worship so heavenly minded that it does not touch us, let alone move us, or, as Coleridge would say, "find us." Such worship springs from a wrong doctrine of Christ and his incarnation. Our worship will give the clue to the inadequacy of our belief. In a full doctrine of the Incarnation there must be

real contact between the God of heaven and the flesh of earth.
That is what we mean by the Incarnation. In the same way as we
can speak of some worship as being so heavenly minded that it
does not even touch the earth so there can be the opposite disease
of a church worship so "relevant" that it never even gets off the
ground. Here again this will reflect a wrong belief about the person of Christ. A church with worship of that kind will be a church
not really living the full doctrine of the nature of Christ—two
natures in one person. For in true Christian worship there is a
living link between heaven and earth, between the sacred and
the secular, between spirit and flesh. That link is Jesus Christ.
Perhaps most of the time we prefer in fact to preserve our schizo-
phrenia and to live between two worlds—generally getting the worst
of both! True worship lifts us and summons us to leave the no-man's
land in which we spend most of our time and to enter one man's
world—the world of Christ in which there is one world larger than
life. That world is the world of heaven *and* earth, of God *and* man,
spirit *and* flesh, in which glory fills all and all is glory. Of course
we shall require new eyes, new ears, and new senses to apprehend
it all for it is a "brave new world" for brave, new men and women.
We shall need repentance, metanoia, and a totally new outlook
if we are to enter the kingdom of heaven, for flesh and blood cannot
enter unless it is in Christ. This was the significance in the early
Church of the custom of anointing the eyes and ears of the new
Christians during the Lenten season before their baptism at Easter.
It was to prepare their senses for the impact of the kingdom. For
true worship cannot end in anything that is churchy. By the *anaphora* we are lifted up as the Church into the kingdom where the
church fulfills its deepest yearnings. So our worship must never
just leave us where we started, but rather lift us to where we
belong—the kingdom of heaven. In his portrait of the saintly Bishop
King, Henry Scott Holland tells of an incident in which the bishop
was instructing a shepherd in a village in the wolds of Lincolnshire.
"He loved one of them, who had slowly learned that the candles
on the altar were lighted in broad daylight, because they had no
utilitarian purpose. They were not there to give light but to bear

witness. 'Eh! Then yours is a Yon-side religion, I see, Sir.' It appeals, he meant, to something beyond this world."[19]

There is a sense in which all our religion should be "yon-side": in the sense that Christ is "yon-side." There is also a sense in which Christian worship should start at *this* side, where Christ's redemptive work began. In living Christian worship we are moved from one side to the other as we enter ever more fully into the mystery of Christ's passage—his passover. Nothing less than this—the closest of all possible associations—between the Christian and Christ's saving activity was St. Paul's vision of the Christian life. Nothing less than this is the scope of full, living, renewed and authentic Christian worship. The doors of the kingdom are stormed at every cry of "lift up your hearts," and wherever two or three are gathered together in Christ, Christmas and Ascension are no longer isolated feasts in the church's calendar, but rather markers at the two extremes of the total spectrum of worship and adoration. God is let loose on earth; man is released into the environment of heaven.

Nothing less than that is the mandate given to the Church in the ordering of its worship, and that is our business every Sunday and "seven whole days not one in seven."[20] The Church is a school for this, the most vital, yet most natural, yearning of mankind— the desire to worship and adore; to enjoy God forever; to enter the kingdom of heaven, even now on earth and to begin to learn while we are still pilgrims in a passing age, the "conversation" of heaven.[21]

3

Worship and the Church Today

THE SPECIFICALLY CHRISTIAN WORSHIP of the Church must be related to the instinct for worship common to all mankind. Although the worship of the Church's liturgy represents a reordering of this instinct in Christ it must not be so elevated or clinical that it fails to pick up what is basic and universal. It must make a positive approach to the folk religion, which is still evident even in western secular society. Perhaps one of the main failings of the Church today is its inability to be "baptized" with that folk religion (albeit a folk religion in grave need of redirection and redemption). The worship of the Church must be first natural and then it can become truly supernatural, otherwise it could end up by being blatantly unnatural. To use the quotation of Paul VI's in the previous chapter, the sacred must not be "contaminated" but at the same time the secular must not be "altered" to the point of being perverted, un-natural, and unrecognizable. The principle of the Incarnation is a continuous principle and process throughout the whole history of the Church and should never be more in evidence than in the worship and liturgy of God's people in every age.

There have been, however, in recent debates within the life of the churches, some prior questions that demand our serious consideration if we are to proceed later in this chapter with some detailed discussion about the conduct of worship and its con-temporary renewal. We need to begin by applying and testing some of the principles of Christian worship we have discussed above. For there are those (strangely enough both within the ranks of Christians as well as outside) who will contest that as God is everywhere there is no place for specific acts of worship specially constructed and located in specific buildings. This conviction has expressed itself in two ways. In the first place there has been the more general and naive assertion (admittedly largely among non-churchgoers and largely in an attempt to excuse themselves from more involvement with the organized church) that has claimed that a God who is everywhere and can be worshipped anywhere does not need specifically to be worshipped somewhere. However contemporary this sentiment may be in its expression, it is an old chestnut! God *is* everywhere, but I am not. God is infinite but I am finite. For the finite creature the opening upon the universal is always through the specific. People who try to recognize God and worship him everywhere generally end up knowing him nowhere. In order to recognize him everywhere we must start by coming to know him somewhere. Perhaps a more homely analogy are those people who fall in love with love: they set out to love everybody but fail to recognize the need to start by loving somebody if they are to avoid the pitfall of ending up by loving nobody— except perhaps themselves! It is the same pitfall and paradox. We may desire to love everybody but we best achieve that end by the specific commitment to somebody. The lesson of universal love is best learned by starting on my doorstep where the most uncomfortable and demanding charity always begins. So it is with our love of God and our adoration for him: he is everywhere, if only we had "eyes to see" and "ears to hear" for "heaven and earth are full of his glory." If I am to recognize him everywhere, however, I must start where I am. Of course, it must not end there, but then we must not in any case suppose that worship either begins or ends with the church service timetable. But that is another question.

The second contemporary debate, which often follows from the assumptions of the first discussion above, is more subtle and perhaps more insidious. It is a contention (admittedly more strongly expressed in the fifties and sixties among many churchgoing Christians and even Church leaders) that is dangerous because it is partly true. It relates to church buildings and their place in the life of the church. Rightly, much stress has been made in recent years on the understanding of the Church as the people of God and the Body of Christ. We have certainly talked for too long about "going to church" rather than "being the Church." The local congregation is the Church: they use a building for the purpose of their corporate worship. Furthermore, the temple made with stones in the New Testament falls under the strongly iconoclastic condemnation of Jesus, unless it gives way to the temple "not made with hands"— those living stones that are the members of Christ's Body, the church. But for some, unfortunately, it is not a very large leap from that kind of argument to the irrational conclusion that if these are to be our priorities in our understanding of the Church, then buildings—and especially expensive buildings—can be dispensed with altogether. It is, of course, undeniably true that in the first two centuries buildings were not high on the priority of a persecuted Church and that wherever Christians have been forced "underground" they have found it perfectly possible to meet for prayer and worship without a building specifically and totally set aside for that purpose. Yet it is equally a historical fact that whenever Christianity has been able to come "above ground" it has swiftly built large, numinous, and beautiful buildings in and through which to express its worship.

We need to reflect upon this indisputable fact because it tells us something about the nature of Christian worship that remains an abiding ingredient in any theology and full understanding of Christian liturgy. Christianity is an incarnate religion and not a purely spiritual religion. Our apprehension of the infinite and transcendent God is *through* the incarnate Christ—man and god. Christian theology sets its face firmly against any attempt to bypass our physical world of flesh and blood, bricks, stones, and mortar in order to leap into the higher realm of the spirit. The realm of the spirit has not split away in Christian spirituality from the realm of the flesh. The flesh is the very vehicle of the spirit and is moved over into the realm of the spirit where it attains its true and lasting significance and glory. So the meeting point for mankind with all that is spiritual is necessarily located within the realm of time and space—most conspicuously and particularly in the incarnate Christ (the Word made flesh). But the work of the Incarnation is always contemporary. This means that spiritual worship is always clothed in matter. Artists, architects, musicians, poets, and dancers have seen the raw material of their craft immeasurably enhanced through worship. The inevitable result is that since the very beginning of the Church's life, an offering spiritual in its goal has never been ashamed to pick up and shape the raw material that is at hand on the way, bending it exclusively to the glory of the spiritual and unseen God. In other words, if you were to pull down every religious building set aside for worship and start again, there would always be artists and stonemasons bent on erecting again buildings that point beyond themselves in what, for the want of a better word, we would have to call worship. It began with Mary the mother of the Lord in her *Fiat mihi*—her great "Amen"—when she offered her body as the ark and temple of the Word. The tradition continued with the other Mary (possibly of Magdala) who worshipped Jesus with the best that she had to offer: "oil of spikenard very precious." Furthermore, we are told that the first "church-building" (possibly the prototype of all future church buildings) was an offering by the "good man of the house" who, when asked by Jesus for the smallest room in the house for the Passover celebration (and the initiation of the Eucharist) in fact offered his "large upper room, well-furnished," the very best that he also had to offer. And so it has been ever since. Worshippers have offered only the best, and that has frequently been the costliest. David in the Old Testament, when he was offered the threshing floor for his altar "on the cheap," pointedly refused the offer with the words: "I will not offer to the Lord that which costs me nothing." Worshippers have frequently embarrassed more cautious souls with their positively prodigal and even seemingly wasteful excesses in the realm of worship and with their desire to give to God only the best for the best. It is not surprising, therefore, that for a truly worshipping Church there is the perennial problem of how to avoid becoming indecently and decadently rich! For the Church has naturally been the recipient, or perhaps more accurately, the custodian and steward, of the world's greatest gifts. This is an inevitable by-product of worship. Perhaps we need to press the advocates of a spiritual and invisible Church (the doctrine of the real absence!) a little further, for there is a good deal that is not only theologically wrong in their arguments but that is not a little bogus. Of course, in many places the local congregation is best housed in a simple and purpose-built church building. Often they are the best churches because they are the small churches built in the shape of a box. That is fine. Yet the argument begins to look less convincing when we see that God's house is made of "wood" while the houses of the congregation are made of "stone." There are frequent cases where a congregation will own their own houses of not insubstantial wealth, and not exactly inadequately furnished, while claiming to believe that God's house should just be simple and, by inference, cheap. What sort of religion and worship is it that can contest for such a glaring dichotomy? It could be, quite frankly, just some convenient double thinking: spiritual (and cheap) for God; material (and the best and most expensive) for self.

This is not to say, though, that we should become slaves to buildings or to the record of history. If Hitler had not destroyed many churches (at least in London) during the war years, then responsible Church planners would have had a very large headache indeed in the years since 1945. The building must be the servant of the gospel and not the master. Many large buildings can be and must be sensitively and imaginatively reordered to enable greater use for more hours by more people for more purposes. Some buildings simply must go—not least in areas of shrinking population. Nevertheless recent experience (and research) has taught us that a church building in any area (even of minimal church attendance) makes a significant and eloquent statement about the soul of that community and should not be lightly dismissed as redundant.

A Church without buildings at all may well be a very spiritual Church and might indeed go a long way to meet the ideals of the young and enthusiastic religious sentiments of our present day, but it would have very little to do with the Church Jesus Christ came to found. Because, in fact, God does not deal with us in a "spiritual" way. When God wanted to express his love for us, he did it in a way that ensured it would show up on the pages of the history book and geography book. He sent his Son, born of a woman, to live at an address and to enter into history as well as to transcend it. Such must always be the double thrust of a Church and Christian presence in a city or in a nation. If God is to have a place in urban society, at least for the present, he must be visible on the skyline, with an address and telephone number. The Church must be visibly and tangibly present (as everything else is present and tangible) in order to create a place of meeting *within* the consciousness of man. W.H. Vanstone writes:

> Man aspires to present an offering of love. . . .This offering is . . .something that actually is. It belongs to the same level of concrete actuality as the stones and trees and stars in which the creativity of God is expressed and completed. As the creativity of the artist is nothing until, through struggle and discipline, it discovers itself in the emergence of a work of art, so the responsive creativity of man to the love of God is nothing until it discovers itself in the emergence of the concrete actuality of the church. The church is not "the cause which the church serves" or "the spirit in which the church lives": the church is the service of that cause and the actualization of that spirit in words spoken, in bodies in a certain place or posture, in feet walking up a certain hill: in stone placed upon stone to build a church, in wood carved into the fashion of a cross: in music composed or practiced, played or sung: in the doing of certain things upon a particular day and the giving up of certain things during a particular season: in the fashioning, out of time and care and skill, of something beautiful, and in the maintaining, out of time and care and labor, of the beauty of it: in the gathering and training of others so that they may contribute to and continue and enlarge the offering: in the going out to others so that they may share the offering: in the struggle of brain and pen to find expression and interpretation for the love of God: in the event of worship which celebrates the love of God:

in hands stretched out for the receiving of Bread and in lips raised
for the touch of Wine. Here, at this level of concrete actuality
is the response of recognition to the love of God: here is the work
of art, the offering of love, which is the church.[1]

So the Church must never be ashamed to begin (like a tree's roots)
low enough and deep enough, if (like a tree's branches) it is to
reach far enough and high enough. As we have seen, though, so
often it has been the fate of the Church to fall between both worlds
and then end up by contacting neither. Worship must either be
natural or supernatural, but it should have no place in the world
of the unnatural and the self-conscious. But it is hardly surprising
that we have erred in giving a proper priority to brick and stones
and buildings in our understanding of worship, because for too long
the Church has not really given a proper priority to the place of
"the flesh"—the outward and visible and tangible—in its understanding of spirituality in general as well as in worship and prayer
in particular.

    For worship is an activity that includes every aspect of the
human awareness: heart and mind, senses and intellect. St. Paul
bids us to "present" our "bodies" as a living sacrifice, holy and
acceptable to God, which is our *spiritual* worship."[2] We can see
how he is using the word "spiritual" here: not in contrast to the
physical but rather as a quality of worship that includes the physical
and ultimately transcends it. Nothing in the human experience lies
outside the scope of true Christian worship. For too long, at least
in the west, and perhaps especially among the Protestant Churches,
worship has been an activity primarily of the mind. It has been
reduced to a process of edifying the mind and informing the intellect. Yet the scriptural commandments in Old and New Testaments alike are as all-embracing as they possibly can be: to love
God with all our heart and soul, mind, body, passions, and strength.
Archbishop William Temple wrote:

    To worship is to quicken the conscience by the holiness of God,
    to feed the mind with the truth of God, to purge the imagination
    by the beauty of God, to open the heart to the love of God, to

> devote the will to the purpose of God. All this is gathered up
> in that emotion which most cleanses us from selfishness because
> it is the most selfless of all emotions—adoration.[3]

And again he insists:

> What worship means is the submission of the whole being to the
> object of worship. It is the opening of the heart to receive the
> love of God; it is the subjection of conscience to be directed by
> him; it is the declaration of need to be fulfilled by him; it is the
> subjection of desire to be controlled by him; and, as the result
> of all these together, it is the surrender of the whole being. It
> is the total giving of self.[4]

So we can clearly see that all Christian worship is intended to evoke
and educate all the ingredients within the human personality. But
does it? We are regimented in pews, restricted either to standing,
sitting, or kneeling, and most of what is going on comes to us
through our ears. So much that passes as worship reflects the
mentality of the lecture room rather than the environment of the
laboratory, the theater, or the book of Revelation. Worship is an
activity involving the whole body—the Body of Christ, seen and
unseen on earth and in heaven. The prayer and liturgy of the universal Church is explicit and unanimous at this point: "Therefore
with angels and archangels and with all the company of heaven."
Nothing less than that is the context of Christian worship. Yet in
practice, in all the traditions (perhaps with the exception of the
Orthodox Churches of the east) worship has deteriorated into something "conducted" by the ordained minister. This has been true
in recent centuries, whether you have regard either to the reformed
traditions, where there is a monopoly of worship by the preacher
with the emphasis on the word, or in the more catholic traditions
where much of the worship is a monologue by the priest. There
is an urgent and pressing need to recover our understanding of
worship as an event and as something *done:* Jesus said, "Do this
. . ." (*poieite,* a plural verb). The worship of the Church must be
the total activity of the *whole* body. So from the earliest times,
the Church spoke of worship as liturgy. It could borrow no better

vocabulary than that at hand in the understanding of the Greek city-state of the ancient world, in which each citizen performed his or her own liturgia. This was the task for which he or she was particularly responsible and best equipped, and when undertaken within the whole community and alongside the responsibilities of all other citizens, completed the many and varying tasks essential to the maintenance of the city-state.

The liturgy was at the same time individual and corporate: it was never individualistic or totalitarian. So it is not a long haul from that healthy concept of worship to those words written by St. Clement of Rome at the beginning of the second century (circa A.D. 96):

> Unto the high priest his special "liturgies" have been appointed, and to the priests their special place is assigned, and on the Levites their special "deaconings" are imposed; the layman is bound by the ordinances for the laity. Let each of you, brethren, make eucharist to God according to his own order, keeping a good conscience and not transgressing the appointed rule of his "liturgy."[5]

For St. Clement, properly ordered worship was an activity of the whole body of Christ with each member playing his part and with no particular member dominating the rest. There was no audience, for all were participants, though not in any democratic fashion but in that most profound and mysterious image of corporate activity, namely the image of the body in which each member functions within an overriding unity. There was to be nothing of the one-man band about real liturgy; it was to be an orchestra. And notice the problem for the early Church in Corinth—a problem to which both St. Paul and St. Clement were compelled to address themselves—the problem of over participation with the resulting discord, rivalry, and competition. Faced with a whole orchestra of ministries, the problem was to maintain the harmony of unity. This healthy kind of ecumenical problem arises only when there is so much diversity that the necessity for unity becomes uppermost in the minds of those charged with the ministry of oversight, the ordained ministry. You do not solve that problem by silencing or paralyzing the orchestra; rather, you seek out that distinctive and subtle charism

of oversight (an "overseeing" that is not "overbearing")[6] that encourages participation and diversification while "preserving" the
unity of the spirit in the bond of peace.[7] So worship for the Corin-
thian Church was an activity in which all played their part. Renewal
in the Church today is marked by a sense of corporate worship
and similarly needs to preserve the unity of the spirit while at the
same time encouraging diversities of charisms and gifts. Time and
space do not permit a further development here of the relationship
between the ordained ministry, which is essentially characterized
by oversight (episcopacy) and all the other "charismatic" ministries
it presupposes. It is only when all the ministries are in evidence
in a Church that the worship can be fully orchestrated. "Clericalism"
was first apparent in its domination over all the other ministries
before it became evident in the "conduct" (that ghastly word) of
worship. Wherever there is renewal it is evident both in shared
ministry as well as in renewed worship. The two belong together.

We need to take the concept of corporate worship even further
and see our worship not only as an activity involving the whole
body of Christ and all its members but also as an activity involving
the whole human body—mind, heart, and spirit. We shall explore
what this means more fully in a later chapter, but at this point
it is important to establish the principle. Miguel de Unamuno writes:
"There are people who appear to think only with the brain, or with
whatever may be the specific thinking organ; while others think
with all the body and all the soul, with the blood, with the marrow
of the bones, with the belly, with the life."[8] Such is the total process
of worship. Perhaps it is not surprising that the worship most
conspicuous for renewal among young people all over the world
is the worship of the Community at Taizé, a little village in the
deep countryside of France, not many miles from the site of the
medieval monastic foundation of Cluny. Each year, hundreds of
thousands of "fringe Christians" are drawn to this remote spot on
the map of Europe by the sheer power and authenticity of its worship. It is out of that experience that the Prior of the Community,
Roger Schultz, writes these words of advice about the place of
the body in worship:

Do not look for a solution that fails to take your humanity into account. Personally, without my body I should have no idea how to pray. I am no angel, and I have no complaint about that. At certain periods I sense that I pray more with my body than with my understanding. Such prayer is at ground level—one's knees bent, prostrate, looking at the place where the Eucharist is celebrated, taking advantage of the silence and even of the sounds coming up from the village. The body is well and truly present to listen, grasp, love. It would be sheer folly to want to leave it out of account.[9]

It is quite clear that we cannot and must not exclude the body with all its senses in the totally involving activity of worship, for actions have always spoken louder than words in every walk of life and there can be no exception to that rule in the realm of what is, at an instinctive level, the most natural of man's activities—worship. The use of the body is an outward and visible sign of the intentions of the heart and mind, as every ballet dancer and actor knows—or forgets at his peril. But, at a more mundane level, we also know that the use of the body for self-expression is true in the ordinary affairs of everyday life. If I am conducting an interview, the position of my body will indicate the level at which I intend to conduct that interview and will also say something of my relationship with the person I am interviewing. If I remain seated, behind a desk, and you are compelled to remain standing, I am implying that you are my inferior and you may well be on the carpet! If on the other hand you are seated and suddenly I stand up and begin to walk up and down the room, there is the chance that I shall be remonstrating and seeking to make a point or even to deliver myself of some lecture upon a topic that has become the burden of my soul. But if I come from behind the desk and pull up an armchair alongside you, the ice is broken and confidence and cordiality would be the name of the game. Truth to tell, the whole of our life is shot through with ceremonial, often unconsciously, but frequently consciously (as at dinner parties). So it would be a strange fragmentation if, when we expressed ourselves before God, we suddenly affected a distaste for ceremonial. So Colin Dunlop rightly reminds us:

Ceremonial is the contribution of the body to the offering of the total man. You cannot really avoid using the body in any communal act of worship. You cannot for purposes of worship contract out of the material conditions in which you live, even if it were desirable to do so. You cannot demand with reason conditions of worship which are "purely spiritual." Even the Quaker must use the organs of speech and hearing. To employ also those of sight, smell and touch; to use arms and legs; all this adds no new principle, except it be the principle of "wholeness"; the use of your entire being in the worship of the creator. Worship is giving to God what belongs to him: all our body, as well as mind and spirit are his.[10]

The use of the body in worship can be far more adequate and eloquent than many pious words. The liturgy of Good Friday in the western Church begins with the three sacred ministers entering the derelict sanctuary in silence and prostrating themselves (flat out) on the bare floor of a stripped and desolate church. There they remain for several moments in silence in an action that speaks volumes of words about all that could never be put into words concerning Good Friday, Christ's passion and dereliction, his crucifixion and death. So in the early Church (as in the book of Revelation) corporate prayer by the whole priesthood of all believers was always undertaken standing. You knelt to plead; you extended your hands to receive; you raised them in blessing or praising. So worship (not unlike a dance) had movement, shape, poise, and rhythm: an excellent cure for the most characteristic disease of worship — the wandering of the mind. Of course your mind will wander if it is supposed to be doing or saying one thing totally out of step (literally) and unconnected with what the rest of your body is trying to say. Like a good oarsman (to use another image) the eye, the body, and the mind must all be saying the same thing, each bringing a discipline to bear upon all the others, if the boat is to move forward swiftly, most easily, and seemingly, with the least self-conscious effort.

Clearly, if the principle stated here is accepted, then there will have to be in the renewed Church with its renewed worship a refusal to attach party labels to various activities and attitudes or

postures in worship. Neither posture, gesture, nor vesture should
degenerate into party slogans within a renewed Church: each should
be chosen because it is appropriate to the occasion and not for
"high-church" or "low-church" demonstrations. Kneeling, a posture
characteristic for so long of papish practices, is now restricted among
many of the churches (including the Roman Catholic Church) to
only a small and penitential part of the liturgy, while standing and
sitting are both encouraged as postures of prayer for all Christians.
We do not seem to kneel as much as we used to do! Somehow
it is all less fussy and yet more meaningful and it is pointing all
the Churches to a unity in their worship representing a far fuller
and richer understanding of worship than has existed in the past
in any of the various traditions. For the unity towards which all
the Churches are being drawn by the Holy Spirit is a unity of fullness and diversity. This should be nowhere more evident than
in the renewal of worship sweeping through all the Churches. It
may not be too much of an exaggeration to say that unity will be
more obvious and its cause forwarded more powerfully through
worship than through any other aspect of the Church's life. In a
renewed act of worship I am less conscious of churchmanship and
party labels than at any other time. It will be in our renewed worship
that we shall discover unity within plenitude rather than in pieces
of paper, jigsaw ecumenism, or schemes and covenanting proposals.
Although it is perhaps true to say that many outward postures with
their accompanying ceremonial represent inward and hidden victories in past battles over doctrine and theology, it is equally true
to say that the theological and doctrinal debate has now moved
its ground and no longer bears the same relation to these attitudes
and postures. There can even be a healthy pragmatism about our
worship today enabling us to experiment, as well as a promiscuous
approach that is ready to borrow the best from all the traditions.
The result should be a fuller expression of worship and, hopefully,
an ever increasing love and reverence for God—the experience
of being consistently *lost* in "wonder, love and praise."

4

Unity and Flexibility in Worship

ONE OF THE CONTINUOUS and continual tensions in the whole of life is the tension between structure and spontaneity, between form and spirit, between what is organized and what is (or at least what appears to be) spontaneous, immediate, and "off-the-cuff." This tension is nowhere more evident than in Christian worship. Our first responsibility, however, is to believe that such tension is healthy and to resist the temptation to let go of either end. After all, in a good tug-of-war, the two extremes keep their feet on the ground precisely because of the tension between the two contesting parties. Cut the rope—release the tension—and both parties will topple over, significantly, into even more extreme positions. In the history of the Church, the tension between structure and spontaneity is most keenly experienced in its worship, and in any renewal of worship this tension must be restored. In the past, and for too long, the tension has been lost and parties have been formed among Christians that have hardened into denominations, polarizing structure over and against spontaneity, championing a rigid formalism versus the spirit and subjective enthusiasm. Perhaps the extremes of this polarization were most in evidence, on the one hand, in the tridentine Latin mass in which every movement of the priest's hands, down to the last detail, was prescribed by rubric, and on the other hand, in the totally spontaneous, spirit-filled worship of Pentecostal Churches.

In a recovery of health and renewal, these two opposites must be brought back together, for, as in the case of a healthy human body, they belong together. It is precisely the *structure* of the spine that makes possible the maximum *flexibility*, enabling the body to respond spontaneously to each situation whether it be to dance, run, walk, or sit. We cannot either be all bones or all sinew. Each relates to the other to give a maximum amount of structure and flexibility. So, we should not be surprised that an amoeba or a jellyfish cannot dance! So it is with corporate worship. Isolated and opposing factions in the Church need to come together in a new interdependence if the Church is to recover a new plenitude and authenticity in its corporate worship. The spontaneous needs what is structured and ordered to rescue it from the tyranny and even anarchy of subjectivity and mere emotionalism.

Before, however, we try to see how form and spontaneity have come together in recent revised orders of service and in much contemporary worship, it might be worthwhile reflecting on the wider convergence occurring in renewed worship today—a convergence of formerly opposite and opposing traditions, now blending together to give an enrichment and authenticity to the worship of the contemporary Church.

"A threefold cord is not easily broken."[1] It is, in fact possible to trace three main strands converging in the life and worship of the Church in the second part of the twentieth century: sacramental, evangelical, and experiential. The choice of these particular labels is deliberate. In the past, varying denominations and emphases have tended to lay claim to party labels that by their very definitions should belong to the whole Church. It might be useful therefore, initially, to cling rather carefully to the particular labelling chosen in this chapter.

The sacramental approach (sometimes exclusively claiming the label of catholic) places its emphasis upon signs and symbols and, as we shall see in other parts of the book, this is valid and certainly has its part to play in any form of corporate worship. Left to itself, however, it is always in danger of degenerating into what we have designated as cultic, appealing only to the emotions but failing to edify and to reach the mind and will. In isolation the sacramental emphasis is not sufficient. Then there is the evangelical witness, with its emphasis on the power of the word in scripture and in preaching. Here again, this is an equally valid emphasis within corporate worship, but if it is isolated and left to itself, it is in danger of being reduced to mere cerebral moralism, powerful in its moral challenge but failing to reach the heart and therefore to charge the affections and challenge the will. The third strand we have called experiential, though here again, in much popular talk, those who would emphasize this particular strand have tended to claim another label—charismatic. The experiential is surely a most important ingredient in worship, emphasizing as it does the part played in our life by the sense of release and the need to be moved and healed through our worship, praise, and prayer. There was a time when many of us were taught to pray simply at the level of duty—almost as we were taught to clean our teeth: something that must happen before breakfast and from which we were not particularly conscious of deriving any satisfaction. In the recent charismatic release within the life of the Church many Christians have come to experience a new sense of worship, praise, and adoration and for this we must thank God. Nevertheless, if this strand is left in isolation, such worship degenerates into subjectivity—a perpetual taking of our own temperature, or worse still, the chasing after particular experiences of prayer and praise such as tongues, ecstasy and prophesy —in fact, a worship that easily turns into something little better than therapy.

The joy of the renewal movement is to be found in the privilege of witnessing to the convergence in our own age of all three of these necessary ingredients. For example, the use of oil or even incense in worship is not necessarily regarded today as high church or popish. Equally, the emphasis on scripture and the place and priority of preaching is no longer a party matter as more and more Christians of all persuasions see the importance of a worship that has within it a strong scriptural element both in the reading of the Bible and also in the expounding of the word. Thirdly, and finally, many Christians today would want to witness to the impact the charismatic movement has had upon their own life of worship and prayer. They may not be necessarily "card-carrying" charismatics, but there is no doubt whatever that their sense of release in praise and prayer (with or without tongues) has brought to all the Churches a deeper and stiller sense of worship and the love of God for his own sake. Now, when we bind all these three strands together in a single cord, we begin to see something of the richness of much contemporary renewal in worship. This convergence of various emphases is bringing a "pleroma" (fullness) of worship, Christian expression, and experience that is enriching all the traditions and carrying them far beyond themselves into a genuine unity of spirit. To emphasize the prime place of the Eucharist, for example, as the characteristic expression of Christian worship is no longer to be divisive. The Eucharist is now accepted by many Christians as the characteristic, but not exclusive, act of church worship. Equally, the innovation of weekly prayer groups has changed the daily complexion of many parishes beyond recognition. At the same time many Christians are returning to the Scriptures and beginning to find in them a new authority and a new source of daily bread for their pilgrimage.

Such is the enrichment increasingly evident in worship today as these three different strands converge. Much of this is made possible in liturgical reform by building into the new prayer books of all the Churches both a place for structure and also a place for spontaneity. The unity and uniformity, however, of our worship today are to be found not so much in words that are said but rather in the structure and flow of the action of the worship. There is much more agreement about what we should be doing, which in its turn has left us much freer in the way we seek to express our worship. It is this uniformity of action and structure that has made possible a new spontaneity at the heart of worship, because liturgy has returned to a healthier understanding that is primarily concerned with what is done before it is concerned with what is being said. Strangely enough, there is therefore probably more uniformity today in Anglican Churches in all the provinces of the Anglican communion than ever there was with the Prayer Books of 1662 or 1928. It is true that there are many more alternatives and choices in these new books, but the alternatives belong to a pattern and structure of agreed activity. For example, the words of the various eucharistic prayers are secondary to the fact that every congregation now knows what is going to *happen* after "Lift up your hearts" even if they may not be certain which eucharistic prayer will be said. It was the new American prayer book of the Episcopal Church that perhaps most clearly drew the attention of all the churches to the primacy of structuring worship in what came to be rather unfortunately termed "the Agenda Eucharist": an agreed structure of activity in worship that enabled and facilitated enormous flexibility in the words said and in the various prayers offered. Nevertheless, the principle remains for all liturgies and not simply for "the Agenda Eucharist." Today, the sensitive pastor has a real opportunity to "tailor" the liturgy, in the best sense of that word, to the particular occasion in hand. It will be increasingly important to make use of this freedom with genuine pastoral as well as liturgical sensitivity, paying real care and attention to the more timid spirits who will need, for a long time to come, continuity with the familiar forms of worship from the past if they are not to flounder and feel alienated by the "new" and by innovation either of language or of activity.

This is all the more important as the Churches once again return to the ancient mandate for worship that demands that all worship should be "at all times and in all places." It is not "high church" practices that make worship truly catholic, but rather the flexibility of a worship-program in a parish where services are literally held at all times and in all places. By and large, all churches still have a long way to go before they really take full advantage of this injunction. "At all times"—but it clearly is not! Worship tends to be at "sacred" and set hours that relate more to the milking habits of a rural community than to the traveling and work habits of an urban society almost two hundred years after the Industrial Revolution. There really is no hidden virtue in calling God's people together for their most important and characteristic activity—worship —at a time that is most inconvenient. Worship should be "at all times and in all places" because it is intended to be for "all sorts and conditions" of people, even for the lazy or laid-back Christians who come to a Eucharist late in the day on the Lord's day (say, at 5:30 p.m.), for according to the New Testament, early or late, they all get the same reward from the same generosity of a gracious master! Instead—and sadly—it is so often at one time (highly inconvenient), in one place (physically very cold and uncomfortable), for one sort of person (someone who has become conditioned to this whole program and who is totally unrepresentative of the wider community). With contemporary work patterns and the increase of leisure patterns, the churches really must become more flexible about times and places for their worship: Sunday morning for some people and Sunday evening for others, Tuesday afternoon for others, and Friday evening or Saturday evening for others still. In order to be corporate, it is not necessary for everyone to be in the same place at the same time. The corporate nature of the Church is not at all like the corporate nature of any other body on earth, precisely because it derives its corporate nature from one body that is not on earth but which is in heaven—even the Body of the risen, ascended, and glorified Lord.

So we must now recover a healthy diversity that is truly catholic in its flexibility. Modern urban society is more like a railway station than a parade ground. If you are to provide for the needs of passengers at a railway station, you need to be on the appropriate platform at the appropriate moment with the appropriate wares and not standing in the station master's office expecting the traveling population to assemble there and to await further instructions! For whenever and wherever a small group of Christians come together to meet, for whatever purpose, worship should have its place.

Worship in a large cathedral, with perhaps a thousand people present, of course has its place, but there is also room for worship in a church hall in an extended Eucharist before an important meeting; in a field with a group of teenagers on a walking weekend of pilgrimage; in a home, as part of the weekly Bible study; or with just two or three people at the bedside of a sick or dying person. In these and in many more similar situations, what will constitute worship *will be an appropriate occasion, appropriately expressed*. In fact that phrase is the test for all good liturgy: an appropriate occasion appropriately expressed.

Nevertheless, it has to be admitted that it is so often at this level that so much of our worship is distorted and fails: not because of the situation or because the numbers are too small or too great, but rather because it is trying to be what it is not and so becomes *inappropriate*. Worship so often falls between all the options and all the varying dimensions open to Christian worship today. We can think of roughly three main categories. We can talk of cathedral, church, or cell, analogous to the Biblical experience of temple, synagogue, and house. Each of these dimensions should have worship appropriate to it. There is the big occasion of the cathedral or rally when we are making a large statement about God's people and their response to God's call through worship. Then there is the local church or congregation, which probably numbers about a hundred or so. There will be an appropriate expression of worship at that level. But finally there is also the cell—the New Testament quorum of "two or three gathered together"—and most certainly there will also be worship most fitted to this kind of occasion. Each time the worship needs skillful "tailoring" if it is to be an appropriate act of worship.

It will be necessary in each case to go right back to the basic structure of the worship and then, and only then, to consider the appropriate additions and externals and the way these should reflect the occasion with both its needs and opportunities. This will require a detailed consideration of dress, posture, ornaments, music, and all the other ingredients of worship. Each should express that occasion fittingly and with integrity. So often, however, this is not the case. The cell seems to be playing at churches and the churches imitating cathedrals. Inevitably this means that what is done is not done well because the necessary and appropriate resources are not at hand. Everything becomes, then, a pale imitation of what it clearly is not. God's worship, however, seeks to take what is at hand and to turn it to the purposes of worship, whether it be the large stone water jars in the first sign at Cana in Galilee or the young boy's lunch at the feeding of the five thousand. It is only

in this way that the connections of which we spoke earlier can
continue to be made in the imagination of the worshippers—connections between what is so often termed secular and everyday
and what we like to keep separate under the title of sacred, holy,
and other. In true worship the sparks fly between these two categories and the barrier between sacred and secular is continually
broken down as language, posture, signs, and symbols pick up all
kinds of impressions and forge all sorts of connections. In one sense,
good worship travels down "memory lane," evoking from the past,
as well as blazing the path to new insights and a deeper sense of
awareness. Everything about worship should therefore be representative in character, from the priest who represents the people
of God as well as the incarnate priesthood of Christ, right across
to all the signs and symbols used in worship. In many ways, if
the worship of the church really came alive, "ecclesiastical suppliers"
would go out of business as we shall show later under the heading
of signs, symbols, and ceremonies. At all events, all self-consciousness must go if worship is to speak with an authentic voice and
with a power that can enlighten the heart, the imagination, the
will, and the emotions, bringing all of these under the Lordship
of Christ and into the presence of the Father.

An inner-city bishop or a bishop with a significant number of
missions and scattered congregations will frequently find himself
visiting churches where the congregation is small in number. But
what brings pain and sadness is not the small number so much
as the apparent inability of those responsible to order the worship
appropriately. From the outset, everything about the worship is
borrowed and imported secondhand from a faded and jaded form
of worship that would have been more appropriate in the setting
of a cathedral-church or "in choirs and places where they sing."
One is therefore not so much conscious of the tiny congregation
as of all the ghosts of what is absent in the worship. It is just
trying to be what it is not. There are perhaps three women and
a boy dressed in strange cassocks and surplices standing apart (in
what are supposed to be choir stalls), accompanied by an in-
competent organist playing an indifferent organ. The congregation

(all forty-eight of them) are straggled all over the place in uncomfortable pews. The service begins with a large and pretentious hymn, played to a large and pretentious tune pitched rather too high for most people who are present—perhaps "Nun Danket" (the well-known German tune to "Now thank we all our God"), which starts with three top Cs! There are two-and-a-half servers, and one of them is struggling to carry a cross at the head of what is parading as a procession, while the vicar (given half the chance, arrayed in a cope because the bishop is present!) is headed by the fragmented choir and servers all of whom enter the church as though it were the vast nave of a European Gothic cathedral. The sermon is preached from the pulpit in a style more appropriate to a State of the Union Address to Congress. The altar, or holy table, has been dressed with faded (though elaborate) hangings and a frontal with a rather over-large vase of flowers uneasily standing to one side. The collection during the hymn is a major operation engaging the only two men from the congregation carrying large dusty wooden plates in which a rather obviously small collection is pompously and pretentiously collected and blessed. A bread board bearing a loaf of bread and a breadknife together with a bottle of special "church" wine is rather uneasily, though self-consciously, carried down the central aisle in what is intended to be an offertory procession although in practice the aisle is only twenty-five feet long between the back member of the congregation and the priest standing with hands extended at the holy table.

Everything, from beginning to end, is "out of key"—plainly absurd. In the first place we should ask why we always need to have the worship of the church accompanied by an organ? If it is appropriate to have a body of people who act as a choir to boost the singing, why should such a choir be dressed up or sitting away from the congregation whose singing they are intended to lead and encourage? Why is it necessary to "preach" from a pulpit when it might be much more appropriate to stand in the center and address the people or borrow a small lectern from which the gospel has just been read? Everything will require re-tailoring if this small act of worship is to ring true and lift those present into the one great act of worship in heaven. In many ways, it is the small act of worship that demands the largest amount of work if it is to be authentic. As in so much else, if we take care of the pennies, then the dollars will take care of themselves. Tailoring worship to the small occasion requires a ruthless eye for detail and the determination to start from scratch and only to add what is needed and what is appropriate. Then, and then only, will the action stand out clearly instead of being lost in the claustrophobia of religiosity, which is perhaps the greatest enemy to true worship.

It is here that so many of the new prayer books, wisely used, can be such useful and flexible resource books. Note, however, that they are resource books and not handbooks and least of all books for the pews. The first requirement, therefore, for ministers of religion and for those who are really concerned with the worship of God is to sit down and read these large and lengthy books from cover to cover. It is important to know what is available and what all the alternatives are, as well as to master the wide range of material they present. There is infinite flexibility because there is a strong sense of structure and shape throughout the services. Furthermore, careful study will show how very little is mandatory. This freedom is not given so that worship will deteriorate into chaos, but in order to preserve a simple pattern and outline that brings its own sense of order. We should not be too ready to add too much extra material (least of all hymns) until we are very clear about the style the worship requires for a particular occasion. Shape, structure, and style in worship should not compete with each other but should belong together in a single integrity.

Then there is the wealth of biblical material readily accessible and clearly available in the lectionaries of all the new prayer books. It is worth sitting down and making your own index of all the various services, readings, and prayers available so that there are ready options for worship on many and varying occasions. Happily, gone are the days of only some twenty years ago, when a priest or pastor could easily get by with three books in the worship section of his library—a bible, a hymn book, and a prayer book! There is now a whole and ever-increasing library of new material for worship, and a wise and sensitive pastor will value a detailed knowledge of prayer books, hymn books, spiritual songbooks, and lectionaries. He will see them as important and necessary resource material, essential for providing living and effective worship week by week. As much of the new music is *not* best accompanied on the organ and as so much music suitable for singing in worship is comparatively new, keen church musicians should not be above taking the trouble to acquaint themselves with the ever-increasing musical repertoire, some of which is most likely to become available through the musical experience of those responsible for conducting worship and assemblies in schools.

All these ingredients require today from priest, people, and musicians alike a vast working knowledge, as well as a readiness to pick and choose, like a "wise scribe" bringing out of our treasure "things new and old." In good worship—as in good architecture—it is perfectly possible and even highly desirable to put strands from differing periods and differing traditions alongside each other. Each strand should be the best of its kind and there should certainly not be any hesitation to use material ancient and modern within the same service. Healthy and living tradition does not need to cut off the hand from the past that can nourish the present. Past and present must together reach out to the future. Surely there will never be a generation that will not require the opportunity to sing the "Veni Creator" to its traditional melody, while also using as a prayer and as a spiritual song the lovely invocation "Spirit of the living God, fall afresh on me." God's people need many of the great prayers of the past as much as they did centuries ago. There must be no doctrinaire or rigid cult of "neophiliacs" who so often seem to believe that renewal is to do with vogue, fashion, and the latest thing. Worship must belong to the age in which it is rooted, but it must also transcend the limitations of that age and draw upon deep and diverse resources.

The next most important area, where flexibility and competence are urgently needed, is non-eucharistic worship, and we must seek out opportunities for such worship. The Eucharist is and always has been the characteristic act of Christian worship: the characteristic, but not the sole act of worship. In the renewal of the Church today, Christians come together on many and varying occasions and in many and varying groups in which they will wish to worship God. It is not only impossible for a priest to be present on every occasion; it is even undesirable. It is the non-eucharistic worship of the community of Taizé, in France, which has captured the imagination of the young Christian world. The simple scriptural office is right at the heart of renewal in prayer and worship in the Church of God today, as it has been in centuries past.

The secret of such worship is not so much that it is non-eucharistic as that it emphasizes—largely through scripture—the baptismal status of a Christian. It opens the hearts of those who worship to the reality of their adoption into Christ as free sons and daughters, sketches out the features of life in the kingdom, a kingdom of love, and joy and peace; praises God in psalm, hymn, and spiritual song; and reflects silently and corporately upon the great promises of scripture. So all those present are enabled to internalize and realize the identity of the Christian vocation.

Here again, structure and flexibility must go together if worship is not to deteriorate into a hymn sandwich conducted abrasively from the front by the parson! We can use a liturgy of the word—the synaxis of the Communion Service or what the Church in the early days used to call the liturgy of the catechumens. The Roman Catholic Church has published a large variety of such liturgies for many and varying occasions, not least its new penitential liturgies. Then there are the daily offices of all the Churches, which are simple in structure yet rich in content and flexible in form. While it is true that it is possible to use the daily office as a personal and individual discipline for Bible reading and prayer, the tradition of the Church has always been to put the emphasis on calling together God's people for this simple daily act of worship. Cranmer was right when, in the Book of Common Prayer of 1662, he stressed the corporate nature of the daily office by insisting that the bells be rung to summon the faithful for corporate prayer rather than leaving the office to be recited and mumbled by individuals in what so often tended to deteriorate into a legalistic and individualistic piety. What is the realistic application of this dimension of worship for God's people in the twentieth century? In the first place, surely it is possible to have a vision of countless small cells of Christians in every parish throughout the land, either of aging widows and widowers, unemployed, or people who work at home who in the pursuit of a genuine lay spirituality see the daily office as the heart-beat of the local church. It can take place in church, but it need not do so. It can be led by the priest or local ordained pastor but need not be so. Where appropriate and where possible it could be sung to simple music. Such a movement of the spirit (for such it would be and should be) would give to the churches a scriptural and lay worship that could be infinitely flexible according to life style, opportunity, and vocation. Furthermore, there could be a strongly vicarious element about such worship. The whole Church, lay and ordained, should ideally be committed to such daily prayer and worship, yet not everyone is free or able to undertake it. Those who are able to do so, worship on behalf of the whole Church as leaven to all God's people, as God's people in their turn should be the leaven for the whole world. Such a movement of the Spirit renews the whole Church and means that worship becomes the most natural of all activities for God's people whenever they come together, whether as "two or three gathered together," or as a large congregation summoned to the church building for a service. It is difficult to think of any more relevant and distinctive way by which the Church today can rediscover its baptismal status, its identity, and its vocation to serve the wider community. Each day the Christian needs to lay hold afresh of that vocation, recalling his baptismal privilege through the solemn and reflective reading of the Scripture, through silence, song, and prayer—a daily diet essential to his well-being and equipping him and sustaining him for witness and work in the world.

Perhaps a word or two is not out of place here about our closed church buildings. While it is sadly true that vandalism increasingly has necessitated the closure of church buildings for six days out of seven, there is a more profound and sad reason for this situation. An empty church building will inevitably fall prey to vandalism, but why is it empty? Could we not still rescue many of our churches by a daily routine of worship, vigil, and prayer? A daily prayer roster would not be impossible to maintain in many of our church buildings at least for a few hours a day during the week. Our churches could once again become shrines, warmed and hallowed and soaked in daily prayer and worship that would condition them, like nothing else on earth, in readiness for the Sunday act of worship. Furthermore, God often gives to a local congregation a strange, odd (and by human standards) perhaps slightly mad man or woman who practically lives in a church building, given half the chance. Such people should neither be despised nor ridiculed. It is not such a bad sign of the quality of Christian life in a congregation to discover just how many displaced people, on the margin of life—and even some who have dropped through the network of life— are "at home" in the church building. We might well be in danger in the twentieth century of writing off either Simeon or Anna who presumably daily "haunted" the temple at Jerusalem, yet it was given to them (as it is always given to such fringe people) to be among the first to recognize and reflect upon the presence of Jesus. A church building is a poorer place without such people in and around its walls. A church that has been locked from one Sunday to the next like a redundant museum is no place to take up the continuous worship of God at a service on Sunday morning. You cannot begin to worship unless you first belong to a community committed to continuous worship. An open church building is a risk, but also creates new expectations, the fulfilment of which might well solve the original problem of vandalism. Problems are solutions in disguise and some problems are of our own making because we have started from the wrong premise. An open church building is a risk, but a closed one is an offense at a very basic and cultic level, even a shock, from which the man in the street has yet to recover in his gut-level reactions to the Churches and the religion for which they are supposed to be in business. An open church building will either be vandalized or used continually for prayer: the problem of vandalism is an inevitable problem in a church that has lost its vocation to pray at all times.

To return now to the theme of flexibility in worship. It will be important to conclude with a few basic underlying principles to guide us and release us into an authentic freedom and unity in the spirit in our worship. It is important to insist that worship will only be authentic to the extent that it is truly *unselfconscious*. This does not mean that it has got to be spontaneous or unrehearsed any more than good dancing has got to be spontaneous. Nevertheless, the difference between a rehearsal and a performance is precisely in this area of unselfconsciousness. The rehearsal is necessarily calculating and calculated: the performance has about it, equally of necessity, an element of "givenness" that opens up the whole dimension of the transcendent.

It has to be admitted, however, that so much of our church worship is blatantly self-conscious. From the moment people enter the church building in their "Sunday best," there is this strong element of man-created self-consciousness. Strangely enough, it is Jewish worship and perhaps also the worship of the Orthodox Churches of the East which seem most able to achieve this blend of authenticity with a total lack of self-consciousness. They are truly supernatural because they are first and foremost natural. "But it is not the spiritual which is first but the physical, and then the spiritual,"[2] says St. Paul, and perhaps this is nowhere more important than in the worship of the Churches. But here we also need to enter a note of caution, for natural is not the same as cerebral, understandable, intelligible, or relevant! For too long the Church has committed itself to scaling down its worship and reducing it in the wrong ways for the wrong reasons. The faulty reasoning behind this reductionism was the misguided belief that unless worship was *understood* it was not authentic. Worship, by definition, cannot be comprehended: it must be apprehended and apprehending and able to take hold of the whole person and take us where we would not necessarily choose to go. It is all right as far as it goes to have the order of service printed out; and in many ways, with a prayer book that is primarily a resource book, and not a handbook or a book for use in the pew, such orders of service are most useful. Furthermore, anything that releases the congregation from the

invasion of a clergyman giving out hymn numbers or page numbers
is to be applauded with gratitude. But let us also try increasingly
to release the congregation (and the clergy) from worshipping God
with a piece of paper or a book in their hands. The words of worship, like the words of a play, are perhaps best apprehended not
so much by following them in print (at least not at the performance)
but rather by allowing the sheer power of words to take hold of
us at all times and at different levels.

It is true that a casual visitor may feel rather lost and there is
something to be said, therefore, for having a simple outline of the
service available (possibly on a card) on request or, when appropriate, at the back of the church. Nevertheless, in reality casual visitors
are the exception these days and cannot be the inhibiting factor
around which all the worship of the Church should be ordered.
And, furthermore, it needs to be said again and again that if the
worship of a church and congregation is rich, authentic, and deep
it will have about it a compelling power, not a thousand light-years
away from the power of evangelism, and will be able to reach out
not only to the initiated but also to the uninitiated and to the
enquirer. Of course, such an enquirer may well need to seek some
instruction at a later stage, but the main point we are seeking to
make here still stands: worship cannot and should not be so easily
and obviously understandable to all that it fails to be a sufficiently
substantial diet for the committed.

The whole relationship today between the Church and society
is vastly different from that which existed in the days when the
English Prayer Book of 1662 was first published. Christian worship
in the last half of the twentieth century is (and is likely to remain
for a long time to come) primarily aimed at a minority of the population. Richard Hooker was the architect of all the political and
social implications of the Elizabethan religious settlement, and at
that time to be an Englishman was the same as being a member
of the Church of England. The worshipping congregation was
neither more nor less than the local community, man, woman,
and child, in their "Sunday best." So, originally, the Prayer Book
of 1662 was public property in the same way as the Highway Code

is public property in America today. Nothing could be further apart than the intentions of the Elizabethan settlement at the end of the sixteenth century and the religious climate in the west at the close of the twentieth century. Hooker's presuppositions no longer apply either in pastoralia or in the liturgy and life of the Church. This does not mean the Church should retreat into a ghetto mentality. But it does mean that as Christians we are free (and should remain free) to see our worship no longer as primarily a service for those who come from time to time, in order to conform to the law of the land, but rather as a whole way of life, expressing all that it means to be baptized into Christ and to belong to the kingdom. Increasingly, people today are members of the Church before they come to church. This should bring to the churches a greater liberation in the style and content of their worship than we have known for many centuries—possibly since the days of Constantine when Christianity began its long, and now almost completed, chapter of being an established religion.

There will be, and there should be, times when worship is informal—informal but never trivial, however. There is a place for right informality, an informality arising naturally out of the kind of occasion in which the worship is taking place. The preaching and the praying will be very different in style in a large building with several hundred people present and in a house communion or a small prayer group consisting of a handful of people. Nevertheless, there must be about all our worship, whether in cathedral, church, or cell, the ultimate sense of God's presence, the *mysterium tremendum*, for worship is an encounter with God and with reality in a way that so much else in our daily life clearly is not. Therein lies its authenticity. It seeks to speak to the whole person and to lift us out of ourselves in an act of self-transcendence. Worship will necessarily include the ingredients that speak to our minds and to our wills, but these will belong to the larger and fuller process of transcendence and coherence. Informal, then, but never trivial; supernatural, but never unnatural; tailored for the immediate but never trapped in the relevant and the banal. Above all, worship is both structured and spontaneous. Like a skillful dancer, it balances these two qualities in interdependence; like a bird in the heavens, it is lifted on the wind of the Spirit.

5

Music and Worship

MUSIC AND WORSHIP have always belonged together and at its best this partnership has been a partnership of complementary roles and not a competitive struggle. For music is essentially the bicycle of the liturgy. "From experience, men have found that music not only kindles the imagination but serves as the most practical vehicle of corporate utterance."[1] So one writer expresses the close affinity between music and the surge of the inner life of man:

> Music is thus not only closely related to life by its power of personal utterance, but still more by its essential character as rhythmic flow; for our life is a continuous movement, of which we are conscious through periodic recurrences of experience. Life is never a state, but always a process; never a being, but always a becoming. Of music alone among the arts is this wholly true. The dream and the dance possess rhythmic flow in varying degree, but they remain external to all but the participants. Other arts are static in their relation to the life of man. Architecture permanently shelters and expresses the various manifestations of his social activity; painting records his interpretation of the world which he sees; jewelry and clothing adorn his body; sculpture perpetuates the forms of that body in its more perfect or passionate states; poetry delineates the particular aspects of his thought and feeling. Only music moves and changes as his whole being moves and changes, lives parallel with his life, agonizes with his struggle, mourns with his grief, exults with his joy, prays with his adoration.

From the far dim dawn in barbarism of that 'light which lighteneth
every man that cometh into the world', the sense of divine vision
has evoked the mysterious power of music to express man's reaction to the numinous, to vitalize and supplement speech in the
utterance of worship.[2]

Indeed, the essential relationship between music and worship
is so keenly felt by at least half the Christian world—the Orthodox
Churches of the east—that what we like to think of as a "low mass"
or a "said service" is unthinkable, however small the congregation
may be. And so alien is the idea of worship without music that
ordination to the priesthood in the Orthodox Churches presupposes
at least a reasonable ability to sing. This is no mere preference
of one part of the Christian world. It reflects a deep conviction
about the very nature of worship and the essential condition of
those who worship. Worship brings release; it is the expression
of those who have been set free from the bondage of self-consciousness. In that release, song and music are as inevitable as laughter
at a comedy and as closely related to each other as tears are to
tragedy, sorrow, and sadness.

In fact this has been the basic attitude and outlook of all the
Churches at times of renewal. It might not be too much of an exaggeration to say that there has never been a renewal in the history
of the Churches unaccompanied (literally) by a musical expression.

From the moment when Paul and Silas in Macedonia sang hymns
together in prison at midnight[3] and were dramatically "released,"
there has been a long and continuing story of release and renewal
in worship through hymns and psalms and spiritual songs. We find
a similar scene in Milan in the fourth century. Bishop Ambrose
of Milan, locked and beseiged with his people in his basilica during
Eastertide, began to sing and compose beautiful hymns, some of
which are still sung to this day. By the beginning of the seventh
century the Church possessed the fruits of the Gregorian reforms in
the Gregorian chant of the Antiphonale Missarum, which some consider the most perfect of our inheritances from antiquity, in any
art. It represents a drawing together of the best of three traditions in music: the Greek, the Latin, and the Hebrew; the three

languages that headed the cross of Christ and the accusation of Pilate. The Hebrew element picked up the psalmody from the Jewish temple worship. It reflects the continuity that we see in Acts between Old Testament and Jewish worship and early Christian worship. The liturgical psalms were sung in three parts in temple worship, and at the end of each section the great trumpets were blown and the congregation prostrated themselves before God. With this gorgeous and elaborate ceremony, Christian psalmody has very little in common today except insofar as Christians stand to sing the Gloria at the end of each section of psalms and in some traditions bow their heads as they directly address the Holy Trinity. But there are distinctive elements in the singing of Hebrew psalmody worth noting. The congregation, for example, repeated the first verse of the psalm after each verse was chanted as a kind of antiphon, and, according to the Mishnah, on special festival days when the Hallel psalms were sung the people broke in with hallelujah after each clause. Thus there was established in the Hebrew tradition of worship the important principle of a congregational refrain punctuating the elaborate singing of the choir. Furthermore, there is strong evidence in our Hebrew tradition of the use of the themes and tunes borrowed from local folk songs and incorporated into the worship of the psalms in the temple at Jerusalem. In Isaiah, for example, there is a direct quotation from an ancient vintage song: "As the wine is found in the cluster, and they say, 'do not destroy it, for there is blessing in it.' " The melody for this folk song, "Do not destroy it" (Altashhîth) is prescribed as the tune and setting for the singing of psalms 57, 58, 59, and 75.

The second of these influences, the influence of Greek music upon the Christian musical tradition, is admittedly rather slight. Bishop Athanasius gave certain directions to the Church in Alexandria concerning principles of Church music because the Greek insights supplied what we have come to call the diatonic scale, a form of alphabetic notation later used in the west. Probably we have also inherited some of these Greek melodies.

The Latin influence upon church music in general has, however, probably been uppermost and more lasting by its emphasis upon accent and rhythm. So St. Augustine, the great bishop and doctor of the Western Church in the fourth and fifth centuries, in his unfinished work *De Musica* defines the nature of accent and rhythm and later even writes his "psalm against the Donatists" in a rhythmical style. The "cursus," not named as such until the early Middle Ages, regulated the word rhythm at the end of sentences and gave to music that congregational element that comes from an easily grasped sense of rhythm, accent, and shape.

By the seventh century the three elements, Latin, Greek, and Hebrew, created the Gregorian repertoire of music suitable for use in Christian worship. Music by then was an integral part of liturgy and worship and not a decorative addition. Furthermore, it was never individualistic, but represented the voice of the whole church. Each member of the congregation could join in the active praise of the whole church in accordance with his own degree of musical skill. The congregation would be supplied with refrains and simple melodies (frequently folk melodies) suitable to most people's ability, while the choir or solo cantors were free to exercise more elaborate tones according to their particular skills. The music was, however, always subordinate to the sacred text and was the servant of the worship. No phrase or word was repeated for the sake of musical expedient. In all these ways, certain principles and checks and balances emerged, and for a while held sway amongst all those who were concerned with worship and the place of music within that worship. So,

> This corpus of the strictly Gregorian music at the beginning of the seventh century is the most complete artistic treasure bequeathed to us by antiquity. . . . It is the world's primary treasure of wholly artistic melody. . . . The perfect, the unmarred choral song of the seventh century after Christ, uplifts the mind into a perennially vital expression of worship directed to the one true God, as revealed through his eternal Son in words inspired by the Holy Spirit.[4]

Nevertheless, it is easy to see how from time to time in the history of music in worship over the centuries this balance has been lost and these principles distorted. The music all too easily became an end in itself and the words were lost in musical elaboration. Furthermore, the choir tended from time to time to dominate all else and aesthetic pleasure became an end in itself while the man in the pew was left to his own devices, unable to open his mouth in the music of the worship. It was against this kind of distortion that the Reformers in the sixteenth century set their faces. Merbecke rigorously adhered to the principle of one note to one syllable; and the Lutheran reformers returned to the chorale with a place both for congregation and choir, according to the ancient principle of the antiphon. Other Reformers took the principles of rhythm as an important and practical method for including the congregation in the singing of the psalms and adapted the words to a meter and rhythm that made congregational participation easy and strong. Again, in the Wesley revival, we find music in the shape of popular hymns. In the Evangelical and Oxford revivals of the nineteenth century, the Moody and Sankey revivalistic movement, and, right up to our own day, in the charismatic and other contemporary movements of renewal, the hymn and psalm and spiritual song have an important position and are very much the property of the congregation.

In such a brief and wholly inadequate survey of the story of music in Christian worship, we can perhaps see how some musical elements in contemporary renewal belong to a long and well-tried tradition. Firstly, there is the balance between those with particular musical skills (the choir) and the rest of the congregation. The psalms set to the lovely melodies of Père Gelineau in France in the 1950s reaffirm the principle of the popular congregational antiphon punctuating the more elaborate and more sophisticated singing of the psalms by the choir. The chorus or refrain is a well-tried principle that maintains a proper balance between the choir and the congregation in worship. There is room for further application of this principle in other prose sections of the liturgy and not least in musical settings for the Eucharist. Then again there is the principle of rewriting prose passages in a rhythmic form such as we find in the very excellent rewriting of the psalms in the well-known and well-tried edition of "Psalm Praise."[5] The singing of passages of prose scripture is also part of the tradition, quite wonderfully rediscovered in much charismatic worship and especially well in publications such as "The Sound of Living Waters."[6] In this example, however, we are not so much dealing with hymns or psalms as that third category of spiritual songs: songs sung quietly and reflectively in the release of the spirit. The singing of scriptural passages has always been a strong element in the tradition of Christian worship, for example the singing of the Gospel or the dramatizing of the Passion Gospel on Palm Sunday and Good Friday. It is a wonderful way for the ordinary person to internalize the word of God and to take phrases and sentences from the Bible into the heart where they can form a really effective prayer of the heart—the effective prayer that is such an important part of prayer and worship.

Indeed, it might be possible to draw a distinction, however tentatively, between the singing of hymns and the singing of spiritual songs. Hymns are frequently rather boisterous and often it seems right to stand up to sing the good strong hymn. But the spiritual song is something much more sensitive and subtle, even more intuitive, and is often best sung kneeling or just sitting, sharing in a quiet melody of the heart. Such a song is less strident than a hymn and can form a wonderfully reflective and prayerful part of the liturgy. It is essentially the song of the heart, and when sung by a large congregation forms an especially tender and beautiful environment of prayer, worship, and praise.

Singing in tongues is equally beautiful and is a thousand light-years away from the hysteria of a revivalistic meeting. Properly used it is beautifully resolved with its cadences and its bewildering harmonies. It is very much music though music not quite like any other music on earth. Such music must have its place in living liturgy, though it must belong within a structure and also in the wider context of formal and professional music. In any one service it is important to get the balance right between these various musical ingredients. There must be room for a well-sung anthem or motet in choirs and places where they sing, as well as for the singing of strongly structured and well-known hymns, firmly accompanied.

There is also room within the same service for more reflective spiritual songs and even for singing in tongues when and where this is given by the Spirit and where it is appropriate. There is no reason why there should be rivalry between the professional musicians and other members of the congregation. In a well-ordered service there is plenty of room for varying musical ingredients.

Nevertheless, we must now tackle what has become a very difficult and thorny question in the life of the church. I refer to the place of the choir and the organ and the organist. If we are honest, the choirs and the organists of our day constitute a real problem and even a positive hindrance to the whole of renewal in Christian worship. Those are strong, and perhaps some people would say unfair, words and they are clearly not universally true. Nevertheless, they are sufficiently true to be of real concern among those who are committed to the renewal of the worship of the Church and to the place of music in that renewal movement. The root of this difficulty is the insistence by many organists and choirs of trying to be what they clearly are not. Of course, in a cathedral or large parish church, the organist and a robed choir still have their part to play, and it is an important and vital part. It is equally important to say, however, that in other places of worship such as a small inner-city church, a mission church, a church hall, or even a small worship group, choirs and musicians destroy appropriate and authentic worship. "From the strictly practical point of view music becomes more of a necessity, the larger the building and congregation, as it alone can ensure unanimity"[7] (The more frequent use of loud speakers may, however, nullify this statement). The place of organs and music is largely related to the size of the occasion. And wrongly used they are totally out of place and a great hindrance to Christian worship.

The organ has had a notoriously checkered history in church music. It is such a magnificent instrument that it easily becomes the dominating tyrant—literally a one-man band. The musicians' gallery was, for part of our history, a far more worthy, less individualistic and more strongly local contribution to Church music and Christian worship. Little wonder that the Puritans, for a host of reasons (some good and some bad) were strongly opposed to organs in churches and for a while they banished them altogether from church buildings to the more secular atmosphere of pubs and taverns. Here they soon became very popular for musical occasions that were the forerunner of the music hall! Yet—again "in choirs and places where they sing"—the organ is the right and appropriate instrument for the liturgy of the Church. In all these matters we need to be flexible, able to tailor the music to the occasion, building, environment, and congregation. In certain situations a good and sensitive pianist accompanying from a piano provides a far more authentic and appropriate form of music than any accompaniment by an organist. Equally, the guitar or the flute certainly have their place in Church music, depending on the occasion.

If this is true of the organ and the organist, perhaps we need also to raise some question marks over robed choirs. The Royal School of Church Music, The Hymnal Society, and the Association of Church Organists have done great and valuable work in raising the expectations and standards of ordinary church choirs in town and country, but their success also constitutes a danger. The robed choir, with head choristers and medals, well drilled and well turned out in cassocks and surplices, has its place, but I suspect it is less of a place now than in our recent past history. Small congregations and living cells of Christians meeting for worship will become an increasingly important ingredient in the whole life of the renewed Church and in such places there is little place, if any, for the robed choir. In fact, few things can hinder a small occasion of worship more than a fixation with robed choirs, organists, and all that goes with that kind of liturgical mixture. It is pathetic to see an otherwise perfectly edifying service in a church hall with about twenty or thirty people present at which the organist, seated at the piano, insists on wearing a hood and gown and where there is a straggling procession of four girls, two boys, and three women clad in cassocks too long or too short, minus several buttons, and surplices of varying styles and indifferent cleanliness. Everything is then a misfit. Frequently the arrival of the local bishop on such a scene will goad the choirmaster and choir to attempt an anthem! It will be a rather well-known one from some recent royal occasion. Everything rapidly deteriorates into a kind of Monty Python version of worship at St. Paul's Cathedral, Westminster Abbey, or The National Cathedral in Washington!

One serious word, however, about choirs and professional church musicians. They are a very important part indeed of the life of the whole Church. Music well done is a very powerful ministry and these people share in the priesthood of all believers in a very special and powerful way—so powerfully that all church musicians must be convinced that they belong to the whole body. They must not be allowed to become separated into an alien unit. Much will depend upon a good relationship between the pastor and his musicians. If there is a breakdown of trust here it will soon show up on Sunday mornings. The good pastor will pray with his choir and take care of them. He will take trouble to explain the shape and direction of a service and the place the music has in that overall strategy. He will spend time with the organist or director of music making sure that they share a similar vision about worship, its shape, and the place music should have in that worship. Once the musicians are allowed to become an alien group, cut off from the rest of the Body, then there will arise an unhealthy rivalry between the congregation and the musicians; and the pastor must bear most of the blame for this.

Frankly, it is sometimes far better to start preparing a service without any musical ingredients whatever. Start from scratch. It is bad to construct a service reasoning, "When in doubt sing a hymn." It is worse, when something of doubtful significance is happening in the liturgy, to cover it up with a hymn—and fatal to try a procession!

The scene is a small mission church hall in the inner city. The total congregation of between thirty and forty people are arriving for worship. There is no organ or organist, but a concealed tape recorder is playing through good loudspeakers Albinoni's "Adagio." The people are sitting rather quietly on arrival for there is no way of kneeling in such a setting. The priest enters from the side and the people stand for worship. There is no entrance hymn. After all, there is no nave and no entrance worth making a fuss about. After a moment of silence and stillness, the priest says the opening sentence of the liturgy for the day and so the worship begins in an atmosphere of stillness and reflection. After the epistle, a single voice starts a well-known spiritual song and the people, still sitting, join in quietly and reflectively. A well-known hymn accompanied on the piano is sung by everyone during the offering of the elements of bread and wine. After Communion there is a time of stillness during which the small congregation and the priest remain sitting while a spiritual song begins again without any accompaniment from the congregation. The service concludes as it began in still-ness, and after the dismissal the people sit on for a moment in si-lence before breaking up for a time of fellowship at the back of the church hall where there is coffee or tea and an opportunity for that other apostolic ingredient in the life of the Church, fellowship.

Such a service in such a setting requires neither organ, organist, choir, cassocks, surplices, servers, pulpits, or kneelers or any other such encumbrances. Of course it could be argued that such a diet of worship, if unrelieved by larger occasions of worship, would be deficient, and a congregation like this should perhaps from time to time "go up" to the cathedral or to the local "temple" for the bigger occasions. Nevertheless, such a service in the local com-munity is perfectly edifying and well able to build up the people of God in the life of the Spirit through prayerful worship. Further-more, worship in such a setting carries with it an integrity of pre-sentation. It is not trying to be what it evidently is not: it is not a cathedral, but it is no less authentic because of that. It is a living cell of Christian life without pretensions or apologies for its existence.

Of course there are many other situations where the organ with a well-robed choir has its rightful place. Nevertheless, here again, if renewal is to be the order of the day, all the presuppositions about music need to be reconsidered. Start by stripping the structure of the service down to the bare bones and to the essential skeleton. Only after that rather austere process are you ready to see what is appropriate. The most important ingredient will be the choice of hymns: the right hymns with the right tune. In a church which shall be nameless, the bishop was visiting for a confirmation service. He entered the large and impressive church from the west door to a church full of people and processed behind a large and impressive choir and procession down the nave to the sanctuary where he was due to be seated at the beginning of the service. The opening hymn was a fine one: "Let all the world in every corner sing." What better start to a service? Unfortunately, however, the hymn— fine though it is and even finer with a descant in the second verse— only has two verses. The hymn ended, but the bishop, at the rear of the procession, was still only a third of the way down the center of the nave. So for a further minute or so—in awkward and self-conscious silence—the choristers shuffled rather noisily to their stalls and the bishop made his way to the sanctuary. What a start! When the incumbent was asked why such a short hymn had been chosen for the opening procession, he retorted rather indifferently that he had not chosen the hymn at all. The organist had chosen the hymn for the purpose, the Rector himself admitted, of getting the choir off to a good and impressive start with the "glorious descant of the second verse." Such is a case of the tail wagging the dog and, worse still, of there being no connection between the tail and the dog. The work of tailoring the liturgy in a large church or cathedral is the joint discipline and skill of priest and musician, each working to a common end—the glorifying of God and the building up of the congregation in worship, prayer, and praise.

It is a skill and a lifetime's work. The sensitive minister of religion will acquaint himself with the many dozens of hymn books that are now available. He will probably have a whole shelf in his study given over to nothing other than hymns, psalms, and spiritual songs in various settings and with various tunes. From his detailed knowledge of a rich supermarket of varying musical opportunities he will, in consultation with the readers, the musicians, and the leaders of worship, style with great care the liturgy for a particular Sunday or a particular event in a particular place. This, together with his sermon preparation and background reading, will form a large part of his working week. After all, a priest is primarily a minister of God's word and sacraments and that work properly undertaken will easily take care of a large proportion of his working life. To tailor the worship of God's people in this sensitive and imaginative way is a grave and joyful responsibility that we treat lightly at our peril.

So we must conclude, as we began, with the picture of music as the bicycle of the liturgy: a handmaid but never a tyrant or an end in itself. "No valid church music was ever made merely to be listened to as a sensuous pleasure."[8] That is true, and yet great music well performed and dedicated to the glory of God will always have its place in Christian worship. There can be little doubt that our cathedrals, renewed and rightly used, will be at the vanguard of Christian renewal in our age. "Small is beautiful," but small must also be balanced by large centers of excellence. Cathedrals have a great future. The cathedral is the mother church of the diocese and brings a larger perspective to congregationalism, that particularly prevalent disease, especially rampant in the Episcopal Church of the United States. Deans have more potential as leaders of renewal than bishops. Like Taizé, cathedrals could increasingly be shrines and centers of renewal that people will travel to see and to experience. The small, when it is authentic, will create an appetite for the larger statement, the quest for the *mysterium tremendum*, the holy place, the center of pilgrimage. In such places, although there will be rounds and choruses (as there are at Taizé) and many other dimensions of music, there will always be a need for the agency of professional and well-trained choirs and highly skilled church musicians. That is costly today, but it will be a necessary cost in a diocese in order that God's people may have the larger and richer experience of worship through membership of the worldwide Church.

The cathedral as the seat of the bishop should also ideally be the center of Christian catechesis, training for ministry, lay and ordained, and many of the other aspects of renewal in the life of the contemporary Church. Music will have its essential place in that curriculum, not as a model to be imitated badly in every other church, congregation, and cell throughout the diocese, but precisely because what it has to offer in the cathedral is different from what is available, possible, or practical in smaller buildings with fewer resources.

In many and differing dimensions, music is once again making its mark in authentic worship. The good news of the Christian gospel was heralded by a chorus of angels singing. The handmaid of the Lord herself broke into words that have subsequently and significantly become the gospel song of the redeemed, who, like her, acknowledge "the greatness of the Lord." From vast choirs with major orchestral accompaniment to simple folk tunes as settings for scriptural texts, music has formed the texture of Christian witness and worship throughout the ages. Doubtless it will continue to do so until all our earthly worship is finally subsumed into the worship of heaven, where surely music in some form or another—a form appropriate to its resources and environment—will have its eternal place.

Signs, Symbols, and Ceremonies

L IVING WORSHIP AND TRUE LITURGY are essentially the gospel in action—an action that, like all actions, has the terrifying potential of being able to speak louder than words. In ordinary everyday life, we rightly regard actions as significant and much of our life is fashioned by signs, symbols, and strange little ceremonies heavy with meaning. From the ceremony of inauguration of a new President to the Olympic flame, from the breaking of a bottle of champagne when launching a ship to the passing of a loving-cup at a ceremonial dinner, our everyday life, and especially our corporate and national life, is littered with outward and visible signs and ceremonies intended to convey inner meaning. In some ways they are a kind of shorthand, quickly conveying what it would not be easy to put into words. Or, and perhaps more important, the apt sign, symbol, or ceremony is eloquent when words would fail or seem trite, banal, or just plainly insensitive.

So it is with the liturgy and worship of the Church. The signs, symbols, and ceremonies of worship are intended to convey in outward form the interior meaning and experience of the gospel. Furthermore, this gospel in its turn addresses itself to all the senses in man in its challenge to bring out a total and all-embracing response. *Wachet auf* ("wake up") is not only the cry of Advent but it is also in a real sense the central challenge of the whole gospel. "The glory of God is man come alive," said Irenaeus. In the words of Isaiah it is the opening of the eyes to see and the opening of the ears to hear, the loosening of the tongue, the leaping of the lame and the speaking of the dumb that are the significant signs of the gospel and the kingdom.[1] It is not insignificant that when John the Baptist sent from prison to enquire whether Jesus was the Messiah, Jesus told John's enquirers to observe the signs of the kingdom and to report back to John the Baptist what they had seen in fulfillment of Isaiah's text.[2] For the Bible contests that fallen man is only half awake and half alive. We are deaf, dumb, and blind to God's glory in our midst so it is little wonder that God needs the sign language of sacraments to convey to us his love. Furthermore, the good news God seeks to convey to us at every turning in the road and by every means at his disposal within his creation must address itself to all the senses in mankind: touch, sight, smell, sound, and taste, if that message of love and redemption is to take hold of mankind in the deep recesses of our imagination, "It is in and through symbols," wrote Thomas Carlyle, "that man, consciously or unconsciously, lives, works and has his being; those ages, moreover, are accounted the noblest which can the best recognize symbolic worth and prize it the highest. For is not a symbol ever, to him who has eyes for it, some dimmer or clearer revelation of the godlike? Of this thing, however, be certain. Wouldst thou plant for eternity, then plant into the deep infinite faculties of man, his phantasy and his heart."[3] Worship must indeed be able to plant in the phantasy and in the heart if it is to draw mankind godward and to tease men and women away from self-obsession and self-centeredness.

So in that sense, all worship must be catholic—able to speak to the whole man, all mankind, and at all times. Words are just not sufficient for this huge and total challenge. The Bible itself is rich from cover to cover in images, signs, and symbols for it addressed itself in the first instance to a people who were happily less sophisticated than we are today and yet a people who were nevertheless more sensitive and open to the power and influence of the symbolic. "The unseen creator makes himself known through things which can be seen and heard, touched and smelt, tasted

and eaten."[4] It is not surprising therefore that a prophet in the Old
Testament would act out a sign or ceremony. His message was
not only conveyed by words but by actions—and often dramatic
actions at that.[5] For the prophet had the dangerous but important
task of getting under the skin of people, where it irritated and
challenged most. Our worship cannot afford to be less powerful.
Good worship is not just superficial; neither is it merely cerebral
and educational. It must have about it that dangerous potential
to get under the skin, to irritate, to displease but also to move
and to challenge.

It is true, of course, that sometimes ceremonial signs and symbols are counterproductive because they draw attention away from
God by focusing on themselves. Symbolism can become obscured
and tamed by aesthetic considerations until it actually distracts from
the message it is seeking to convey. So it was that by the fifteenth
century the ceremonies of the Church in the west had become
so decadent that it was scarcely possible to see through them: the
icon had become an idol; the means had become an end. It was
against that background that the Puritans became so iconoclastic,
seeking to tear down all that hindered plain speaking. They wanted
their worship to be clearly and only rooted in the spoken word
of the gospel—pure and simple truth (in danger of forgetting, as
Oscar Wilde has aptly said, that truth, like love, is seldom pure
and never simple!).

For the truth about all of us is that we are complex in our make
up, but catholic by nature, using all our senses to explore the world
around us. Just stop and watch a baby playing on the floor. Every
visible object receives fascinated and wide-eyed attention. Everything has to be touched, shaken, even smelled. And, as if this were
not sufficient, the object under examination is always in danger
of being put into the mouth to be tasted, bitten, or even swallowed!
Frequently all this is to the annoyance or bewilderment of those
who go by the questionable title of being grownups. Could it be
that we all begin life as little catholics and only later, when we
have been tamed and trimmed, groomed and inhibited by manners,
etiquette, and the rational claims of a sensible society, become

puritans, restraining our senses—only half alive, partly blind, dumb, deaf, and lame? If so, then the challenge of Jesus to be born again may need to be heeded more literally than perhaps we had first imagined. A born-again Christian may well need to be more aware of his senses as he or she becomes more alive in the Spirit. So with our worship. It needs to recover in some places, and in other places to uncover, the powerful, basic, biblical signs, symbols, and ceremonies that are part of our tradition so that our worship can invade every aspect of our personalities, turning our attention and our total selves towards God with a fascination and preoccupation possibly only equalled by a child in its early months in a new world of light and sound, color and smell, touch and taste.

But this process will always have two principal enemies bent upon restraint and reduction: they are the enemy of the intellect and the enemy of the altar guild! The intellect will always be in danger of playing the role of the spoilsport! It will continually be checking, in an analytical way, whether or not this or that experience "makes sense." Of course in one way there is nothing wrong in that, because it is the responsibility of the intellect to act as a check and balance on the other senses. But that is its proper task, neither more nor less. And it should not claim to be the ultimate and necessarily overriding criterion and tyrant in every case. It is simply an important instrument in an orchestra and the overriding balance or harmony belongs to that more subtle and intangible presence within man of man's own spirit. A man's spirit should transcend all his senses and sensitivities if he is to be whole and wholesome in his response to the deepest experiences of his life.

The second enemy of living and authentic symbols, signs, and ceremonies in worship is, of course, the altar guild. Perhaps, with the organist and professional church musician as close rivals, it is those good ladies of the altar guilds (second only to the parson) who over the years have been most responsible for the emasculation of worship. Probably the reason for this is that scriptural symbols are rather messy and inconvenient. Fire, water, oil, ashes—to name but a few—can soon make an awful mess. It is not surprising, therefore, that before long Christian sacristans began to look around for tame, nice, clean, ecclesiastical varieties of these rather improper and inconvenient symbols. Hard on the heels of the altar guild (for the one breeds and encourages the other) you will find ecclesiastical shops springing up that purport to sell an ecclesiastical variety of everything from bread (which does not even remotely look, taste, or feel like bread) to wine bottled under the label of "sanctuary" or "church" wine. So the list grows, from candles that do not burn too much, fonts that are the size of a tea cup, palms neatly and nastily folded into crosses so that they no longer even look remotely like a palm, all the way to the church furnishings—clean, expensive, no longer in touch with the roots of the original symbol and certainly emptied of all significance. Such manufactured symbols are trite and emasculated, impotent to convey the inner message of the gospel towards which they should be drawing the attention of the worshippers.

Renewal demands that in this area of our worship we be genuinely radical. We must go back to the scriptures and traditions of the Church to find out the inner meaning of each symbol, sign, and ceremony and then look around (and, if needs be, shop around) for the most powerful and authentic, contemporary equivalent for use in the worship of God.

WATER

It is not surprising that there are over seven hundred references in the Scriptures to water or waters, for water is the most basic ingredient of life. It is the very environment in which we were conceived and a fundamental necessity for all life. In countries where it is hot and in desert lands, water is carefully guarded and its use is even legally restricted. Among the aborigines in Australia the watering holes are the holy places and shrines, and to misuse these places or to violate them is punishable with death. It is significant perhaps that in the Bible water appears in the very first opening verses of Genesis as well as in the closing verses of Revelation.

Water is there from cover to cover. In the New Testament the largest number of references to water appears in St. John's Gospel and in the book of Revelation. In the imagery of St. John, water and life go together, for water and life belong together in any case: where there is water there is life; where there is no water life will not last for long. As you fly low over the desert you particularly notice this: where there is water the unbroken arid brown is suddenly relieved by a belt of green on the edge of a river or by a wadi.

Roughly speaking, the long list of biblical references to water can be divided into three main categories. There is water for washing and cleansing; there is water for drinking, for refreshment, and sustenance; and there is the more subtle image of water as a sea, flood, or river through which we pass, in which we can be drowned or overwhelmed, and from which we are delivered and raised up. So it is appropriate that in the order for baptism in the new American Prayer Book there is an eloquent prayer spelling out the many images of water in the Scriptures.

> We thank you, Almighty God, for the gift of water. Over it the Holy Spirit moved in the beginning of creation. Through it you led the children of Israel out of their bondage in Egypt into the land of promise. In it your Son Jesus received the baptism of John and was anointed by the Holy Spirit as the Messiah, the Christ, to lead us through his death and resurrection, from the bondage of sin into everlasting life.[6]

Water also marks an overwhelming experience of going under and undergoing—a drowning—the experience of being out of our depth and all that that means. This experience is the central reality of Christian experience and is the most compelling throughout the whole of St. Paul's teaching.

The theological implications of the waters of baptism are thus simply massive, spelled out in a long alphabet of imagery. In fact, it is not too much to see baptism as the fountain of all renewal in the life of the Church, and yet it is this symbol which the established churches have tended to trivialize almost out of all recognition. The font has become the plaything of every architect, seeking to speak only to our aesthetic sensitivities to the point where the hugely inconvenient and dynamic symbolism of water has almost been completely obscured. This is apparent in the practice of indiscriminate child baptism and the place it still often holds in the timetable of church services, where it is tamed and relegated to the proportions of tea on Sunday afternoons. It is also demonstrated by the way *the* sacrament of all sacraments is so frequently and wrongly administered.

Ideally, the font should be in a proper baptistry that either adjoins the entrance to the church or is a separate building altogether. We should physically, literally, and architecturally enter the church through the baptistry. Furthermore, the concept of "undergoing" and drowning is central to the imagery of baptism and certainly a long way from the pious reductionism of the average sprinkling that so often masquerades as immersion. Perhaps even worse is the practice (so often endured by bishops at services of baptism and confirmation) of placing a plinth at the front of the church with a small flower bowl on top of it containing a glass bowl full of water and piously hoping that this reduced and tamed symbol can "speak" to the imagination in the name of washing, cleansing, and renewing, let alone in the more profound symbol and imagery of drowning and death.

It is, however, refreshing to see in many new churches an architectural commitment to the symbolism of baptism. Sometimes the baptistry is built in the floor of the church making possible the image of moving or living water and even permitting baptism in a fashion akin to that of immersion. A special light is now available that if allowed to flood the font, brings the water in the font "to life" in appearance in a quite remarkable and significant way. These, together with the ceremonial of a solemn procession to the font for adult baptism, can recall the whole people of God to the central point of new life in Christ. It is no bad thing in churches where incense is used to highlight other significant moments and places in the liturgy, to cense the font after it is blessed and before people are baptized in it. The ceremony at the font at the Easter Day Eucharist, if conducted by the bishop at dawn with new

Christians for baptism who have undergone a lengthy catechesis and preparation culminating in a devout observance of Lent, can bring annual renewal to the whole congregation. The font is then genuinely seen as the womb of the new life of the Church, made fertile by the invoking of the Holy Spirit, through solemn prayer, fasting, and vigil. In the liturgy of Easter morning, the procession to the font in which the new Christians are led by their bishop to the waters of initiation is traditionally accompanied by the singing of the age-old "litany of the saints." This sets this great Christian activity of baptism in the context of eternity and within the framework of the fellowship of all God's people living and departed. For baptism in Christ is the watershed of the evolution of the human race, and living liturgy will always seek to do all it can to identify and locate this reality on the map of human experience. It should be recognized, as it is in the prophet Ezekiel,[7] as the huge river of new life, flowing northwards, southwards, eastwards, and westwards from the temple of the presence of God in the historical Christ, irrigating and watering the desert of human history, backwards to the dawn of mankind and forwards to the end of time.

BREAD AND WINE

Whatever other layers of significance may have rightly accrued to the eucharistic act since New Testament times, it is still essentially a meal or a banquet at which bread is broken and wine is drunk. "Man is what he eats," wrote Feuerbach in what he intended to be a very reductionist and materialistic statement. Paradoxically, however, he could not have made a more Christian and sacramental statement. We are what we eat and that is why we eat his body: in order to become his body (as St. Augustine said). Furthermore, as eating and drinking are so very basic to the whole of human life, they have become part of the ritual of civilization, with appropriate ceremonial and habits attached to this daily and (generally) corporate activity of the human race. Places where people have

met to eat and drink have frequently become centers of new life,
new thought, and civilization, whether it be the coffeehouses of
Parisian life or the English public house. It is not surprising, therefore, that helps to express this basic and central imagery of a meal
at the Eucharist must be an improvement in eucharistic worship.
for his habit of eating and drinking with sinners. His Jewish critics
were swift to observe when Jesus went into the house of Zaccheus
for a meal at a turning point in that little man's life. They were
all too ready to comment on Christ's presence at a great feast given
by Matthew on the day of his call and conversion. Most of the
recorded resurrection appearances were when the disciples were
at a meal, and it is not insignificant that Jesus' apostolic com-
missioning to Peter in St. John's gospel is recorded in terms of
feeding and not just as an abstract call to a ministry of preaching
or to the spreading of his ideas. "Feed my lambs: feed my sheep."
Some New Testament critics even wish to build up a whole concept
of the teaching literature of the Gospels around the table talk of
Jesus, so basic was the concept of the corporate meal to the identity
of Jesus and his disciples—the Body of Christ. Everything, therefore, that helps to express this basic and central imagery of a meal
at the Eucharist must be an improvement in eucharistic worship.
Clifford Howell writes:

> We begin from a fundamental meaning: to share food and drink
> with others is to have a meal together. Bread and wine are food
> and drink. Our Lord took bread and said "Eat," he took wine and
> said "Drink." The memorial of himself which he then instituted
> has therefore the form of a meal. In the beginning it looked like
> a meal, had the character of a meal and was experienced as a
> meal by those who took part in it. Why? Because they did in fact
> *eat* by putting food (bread) into their mouths, and then masticating
> and swallowing it. Also they *drank* by imbibing and swallowing
> liquid (wine). These are the actions usual at a meal. They knew
> indeed that what they ate was not ordinary bread (though it con-
> tinued to look like bread). It had become the Body of Christ given
> for them. And they knew that what they drank was not ordinary
> wine (though it continued to look and taste like wine). It had

become the Blood of Christ shed for them. But this knowledge derogated in no way from their consciousness that they were sharing a meal together. They realized that it was a very special meal, a sacred meal, an act of religion and not merely the taking of nourishment. But it was nevertheless a genuine meal. It was, moreover, a unifying meal. The bread brought to the altar was in the form of flat loaves, half an inch or more thick, several inches across. To be eaten, such loaves had to be broken into pieces of manageable size after the consecration. These were distributed. Thus each loaf was shared among several people—ten, a dozen or more. And the wine was in one or more cups according to how many people were present. From each cup a number of people drank the consecrated wine. The meaning of all this as expounded by St. Paul (1 Corinthians 10, 16 and 17) was quite clear. They "got the message" that those who shared in one loaf or drank from one cup became one in Christ.[8]

Sadly, eucharistic symbolism has degenerated, as has so much other symbolism in the Church. The symbolism has become an end in itself and the grit of the symbol, which is intended to fascinate and irritate the imagination, has been worked over to such an extent that it has been lost inside a liturgical pearl—albeit a beautiful and aesthetically pleasing one. In that sense, the eucharistic species is in serious danger of becoming a defective sign. It is true of course that if a chemical analysis were to be made of genuine bread and then of the eucharistic wafers made in convents or by some ecclesiastical manufacturer, the results would be sufficiently alike to enable us to be fulfilling the Lord's command of taking bread. Yet, if we are honest, we have to admit in fact that the eucharistic wafers used in many churches simply do not *look* like bread. So often the "bread" used in our churches for the Eucharist defies all the basic necessities of the original eucharistic images. It is not substantial enough for us even to feel that we are eating it. It just melts! Jesus told us to take it and to eat it. The priest so often has a so-called "priest's" host (a large host); and although he eats it, it is not for the purpose of sharing—on the contrary, it is peculiarly *his* host! Hence much important further symbolism is lost. In churches where white sliced bread is used, the whole image of the fraction, the breaking, is completely lost in a soggy mess of crumbs. There are even churches where only the white small wafers are used for the Communion without the large priest's wafer and then any concept of breaking is totally absent and utterly obscured. It is in these ways that a symbol degenerates when the secondary (and generally aesthetic) considerations leave other, more primary, considerations far behind. When something symbolic has become purely symbolic it is no longer a pure symbol. It is contaminated out of all recognition. Whatever else the Eucharist meant in the New Testament, this basic action of taking bread, giving thanks for it, and then breaking it is fundamental. The manner in which Jesus took bread and broke it so riveted itself in the imagination of the disciples that it was supremely this action that brought recognition in the post-Resurrection appearances.

Having criticized, however, much of the bread or breads frequently used by many churches, it is not so easy to come up with an answer both practical and effective as a sacramental sign. In the case of a small eucharistic gathering in a house group it is perhaps easy to take a round wholemeal bun and use this. It can be broken (it is not cut), it does not have too many crumbs, and it preserves the important symbol of sharing one bread. It is another matter in a church where there is a large congregation, let alone a cathedral where there is possibly a very large congregation. In some places, under these circumstances there is a practice of always using priest's wafers and breaking these into four or six parts. There are also recipes for making large flat round crisp breads. These can be broken conveniently and they taste, look, and feel like bread. There are a few convents today where such large wafers are made, but significantly they cannot cope at the present time with the demands made upon them and as yet the cost of replacing the old machines for making wafer breads (generally in convents) does not make it economically practical.

Although we must not make a fetish out of all this, we must recognize the absolute necessity of recovering authenticity in the basic symbol of the central and characteristic act of Christian worship. So, equally, with the wine, and with the manner in which it is used, at eucharistic celebrations. It should be good wine (mixed with water as in the east) and not ecclesiastical wine (generally rather expensive for what it is) offered in a cup or chalice that looks like a common cup. There are some lovely ceramic eucharistic cups available today and also some simple pottery cups that are most effective in an appropriate situation, and all of these are certainly more suitable than the ecclesiastically-marketed silver-plated chalices frequently made in imitation of medieval chalices. Indeed, at large eucharistic gatherings few things look more un-edifying than rows and rows of silver chalices of all different shapes and sizes on a large altar. (Frankly, they can sometimes resemble grandmother's display of silver on the sideboard on high days and holidays.) Simple, identical pottery chalices are far more telling and are probably best held by the assisting ministers during the eucharistic prayer of consecration rather than stacked in rows upon the altar.

In these and in so many other ways the basic image of the Eucharist needs to be uncovered in our generation, and we need sensitivity to get it right on differing occasions where numbers and locations vary so enormously.

A further consideration of the Eucharist should be the concept of food for the journey. The Passover meal was eaten in haste with shoes on feet and staff ready for the journey. Food for the journey is perhaps best received standing, walking to a communion station in the church, singing together with all God's people as men and women on pilgrimage and on the journey of life. Pious attitudes in the Eucharist are alien to its corporate nature. We shall probably not get this right until we redress the balance between corporate spirituality and individual spirituality. Each has its place. At the moment, "going to church" represents so often the sum total of people's prayer and worship. Naturally, therefore, there is a danger that we try to use the liturgy for all aspects of spirituality with the constant danger of falling between all alternatives. Of course, there must be a place and time for personal prayer of the heart, with silence and stillness, in which various individual postures can rightly be adopted. This is balanced, however, by the corporate expression of worship in the liturgy. Both are needed and they are complementary to each other. They should not be confused. In particular the corporate activity of eucharistic worship should not degenerate into individual piety. Kneeling, as in the Middle Ages, and sitting as in the Reformation reaction, are both distortions. There is happily a return in our own day to a more primitive and basic understanding of the Eucharist as food for pilgrims on the move together, singing as they go, and any practical arrangements (even down to church furnishing and layout) that make this possible should be strongly encouraged—though will doubtless be strongly resisted in the name of "interfering with my communion."

LIGHTS OF THE WORLD

There can be few more basic images and signs in religious language in general, as well as in Christian symbolism in particular, than light and (by implication) its contrasting opposite, darkness. It is worth taking a concordance and looking up all the references to light, especially in St. John's Gospel, where it is an important and recurring motif throughout all the chapters. Christ is the light of the world, and Christians in their turn are challenged also to be lights of the world and to "Let your light so shine before men, that they may see your good works and give glory to your Father who is in heaven."[9] It is significant that in the Early Church the great liturgy of the dawn of Easter morning, celebrated wherever possible by the bishop, centered on the liturgy of Christian initiation—baptism and confirmation. The great vows of the new Christians would be taken as the dawn was breaking and as the light of Easter broke through the darkness of sin and death. So when the neophytes were asked to turn to Christ they would literally turn from facing the darkness of the night to facing the light of the day, from west to east. Furthermore, among the many ceremonies and symbols accompanying baptism from early times, the neophyte would be given a candle as a token that he had "passed from darkness to light" and must therefore henceforth "shine as a light in the world to the glory of God the Father."

Perhaps liturgically light is used at its most powerful as a symbol in the first part of the paschal liturgy, the Easter vigil. Increasingly, the whole Church is beginning to recover the centrality of the Holy Week liturgy in general, but especially the liturgy of the three great days, Maundy Thursday, Good Friday, and Easter Day. These liturgies use every device of Scripture and symbolism to demonstrate the reality of Christ's death and resurrection—the central mystery of our Faith, the pattern of our redemption, and the shape and size of our Christian identity. In one sense the more outrageous and extreme the timing of the Easter liturgy can be, the better. Ideally it should be at dawn on Easter morning, forming the climax of a whole night of vigil. Vigil is central to Christian spirituality and this should increasingly be expressed liturgically. Many young people today have responded to the challenge and opportunities of vigil. The ideal is to tell the story of redemption by reading, songs, and reflection throughout the night. The much reduced seven readings allotted for the Easter vigil, followed by chants and prayers, form a framework of what can be a very adaptable liturgy. A whole night can be spent watching and reflecting upon the story of our redemption (perhaps, for the sake of the weaker brethren, punctuated with flasks of coffee) culminating in the kindling of fire, lighting of candles, and the renewal of baptismal vows. This need not necessarily be restricted to Easter and can well form the focus of renewal movements in parishes and dioceses at all times of the year. All great feasts should be preceded by a vigil: not so much a silent or individualistic one or a vigil just for the pious, but rather a corporate and boisterous activity of all God's people— the children of the light and lights of the world.

The first part of the Easter vigil is essentially, however, the service of light, when we pray that we may share in the light of God's glory, through Jesus, the light of the world. So it is that from newly kindled fire, the large Easter (paschal) candle is lit and carried into the darkened church in front of the congregation. It is held high and is splendidly accompanied by the threefold proclamation:

"The Light of Christ." From this candle, all individual candles significantly take their light, until the darkened church is aglow with the Easter light of Christ's resurrection.

But the paschal candle (if it is really large and held high in procession by the deacon as is the tradition) carries with it also the further symbolism of the deliverance of God's chosen people from the bondage of Egypt through the Red Sea of baptism, into the desert, and on to the promised land. Ahead of them, by night, was the pillar of fire and so the paschal candle should always be a large tall candle realistically capable of carrying this further symbolism so obviously demanded. As it belongs essentially in the context of deliverance and redemption, the most appropriate place for the paschal candle throughout the year should be in a conspicuous position beside the font and it is from this light (always lit at baptisms) that the candles given to candidates should be taken. In every way this central symbolism of the Easter candle must have about it a shape and size that make us able to pray and sing credibly the words of the Exultet: "Rejoice and sing now, all the round earth, bright with a glorious splendor, for darkness has been vanquished by our eternal king."

The singing of the Exultet (if it is sung) must be done very well indeed and it should be sung so boisterously that it could well resemble a dance around the paschal fire. If it is not well sung it is probably best recited and proclaimed boldly instead. It must not become just an ecclesiastical and tamed (even tiresome) plainsong rendering! It is essentially a proclamation with all the fire of the gospel sound about it. Indeed, the paschal liturgy well done is perhaps one of the greatest gospel experiences of the Church's liturgy and is worthy of the greatest possible care in its presentation.

Although the paschal candle is central in our use of fire and light in our worship, the extensions of this symbol are manifold. In the twentieth century, the use of candles or illumination in a church building presupposes the proper use of electric light. With the help of dimmers and framing spotlights, and many other contemporary lighting devices, the lighting of the church building has today very remarkable possibilities indeed. It is doubtful, however, whether light should light up all the building. Properly used it should highlight the important and significant parts of the church building, probably leaving whole areas of the building in softer light or even deliberately in the shadow. Against such a background, candles have an important place and can be used to great effect, for example, to flank the Gospel or cross whether stationary or in procession. A light near icons or religious pictures or statues is also very effective. Thank goodness these things can be discussed today without raising questions about the brand of one's churchmanship. The Protestant community of Taizé most effectively uses small votive nightlights and candles, creating as they do a remarkable environment of prayer and sensitivity—an environment that has brought countless thousands of young people across the face of Europe to join in the worship of the building of the Church of the Reconciliation at Taizé, only a few miles from the site of the ancient monastic foundation of Cluny.

The new Episcopal Book of Common Prayer provides a very lovely evening act of worship to accompany the ceremony of lighting the candles. The opening rubric of the service reads: "The church is dark, or partially so, when the service is to begin." Special anthems (Lucernaria) are provided to be said or sung while the lights are lit, and of course (from the eastern Church), there is provision for the singing of the *phos hilaron:*

O gracious light,
pure brightness of the everliving Father in heaven,
O Jesus Christ, holy and blessed!

Now as we come to the setting of the sun,
and our eyes behold the vesper light,
we sing your praises, O God: Father, Son and Holy Spirit.

You are worthy at all times to be praised by happy voices,
O Son of God, O Giver of life,
And to be glorified through all the worlds.

Such an evening ceremony can then continue with evening prayer, or Compline, the Eucharist, or a simple fellowship meal. It is a wonderful use of a basic and simple image, partially functional

in origin, certainly scriptural in significance, and incidentally powerful and aesthetically persuasive in creating an environment for prayer
and worship. In the Christian understanding of time, the evening
has a very special place. Alexander Schmemann writes:

> Contrary to our secular experience of time, the liturgical day
> begins with Vespers, and this means, in the evening. This is, of
> course, the reminiscence of the biblical "and the evening and the
> morning were the first day" (Genesis 1:5). Yet it is more than
> a reminiscence. For it is, indeed, the end of each "unit" of time
> that reveals its pattern and meaning, that gives to time its reality.
> Time is always growth, but only at the end can we decide the
> direction of that growth and see its fruits.

So for a Christian, the evening service

> does not begin as a religious "epilogue" of the day, as a prayer
> *added* to all its other experience. It begins at the *beginning*, and
> this means in the "rediscovery," in adoration and thanksgiving,
> of the world and God's creation. The church takes us, as it were,
> to that first evening on which man, called by God to life, opened
> his eyes and saw what God in his love was giving to him, saw
> all the beauty, all the glory of the temple in which he was standing,
> and rendered thanks to God.[10]

It is in that context that our evening worship makes scriptural sense
and it is in that context that we light the evening lights in antici-
pation of the dawn, not only of the next day but of the new age
for which Christians are in constant vigil.

A word now about lights and their place in outdoor processions
and services. By and large the established Churches are not very
good at outside worship. They have not learned to deal with the
hazards of worship outside the cozy and constrained limits of a
church building. So often church processions look tame and dreary
because we carry our indoor church furniture out into the wider
environment of the street. A cross in an outdoor procession, for
example, probably needs to be specially made (almost to life-size
proportions) if it is to *register* in the imagination and make a statement about Christ's cross on the wider stage of an outdoor service.

It is no use having ecclesiastical candles bought from ecclesiastical manufacturers if you are to go outside for worship. Nothing less than flaming torches will stand up to the challenge. Burning torches to represent candles are probably best obtained from hardware stores or it may be necessary to go to firms where it is possible to buy well-engineered lights and fires and flames that burn butane gas or other fuels. All this demands imagination and thought.

OIL

The return throughout all the Churches to the primitive use of anointing with oil should be welcomed on the grounds of its scriptural authority. Oil in the Bible generally refers to olive oil, which formed a part of the threefold essential economy from the earth in the ancient world: corn, wine, and oil. Oil was used medicinally on an open wound (Isaiah 1:6 or St. Luke 10:4) and therefore it is not surprising that the Scriptures speak of anointing with oil in miraculous healing (St. Mark 6:13; St. James 5:14). Oil also had a cosmetic use, so that in Luke 7:46 it was expected that a host would anoint his guest at a banquet. In fact, it was the Pharisee's neglect of this apparently expected courtesy that is so devastatingly contrasted with the sinful woman's lavish use of the much more expensive myron (oil of myrrh). Add to all of this the use of oil by athletes in the ancient world (as indeed in our own day), and it can be seen that oil is a sacramental substance, an outward form with a distinctive use that easily points to an interior and deeper significance. For St. Augustine, confirmation was the oil of chrism, an enriching in Christ, so it is good that in some churches today oil is restored for use in baptism and confirmation as well as for anointing the sick and anointing, for further chrismating, on occasions of renewal and rededication.

It is appropriate that the oil used in the diocese for any of these ministries should be blessed by the bishop, especially on the occasion of the re-affirmation of priestly vows on Maundy Thursday. In the whole extension of our understanding of ministry, diversified

yet unified under the oversight of the bishop, the healing ministry
has happily been placed high on the agenda. To be anointed nowa-
days is not regarded as necessarily the same thing as receiving the
last rite, but rather as a further strengthening and refreshing for
the pilgrimage of faith. Seen in this wider context of ministry,
anointing with oil can be used at the end of a parish mission and
indeed at all times when there is a real reaching out to further
commitment to Christ and a further chrismating of God's people.
It should never be allowed to deteriorate into a fancy "high church"
ceremonial but should always have about it something of its robust
Old Testament character. It is the anointing of God's people to
be a priestly people, a royal priesthood and a dedicated people,
a prophetic sign of God's desire to set his people apart for their
royal and priestly responsibilities and vocation in the world. It is
also a vivid reminder that Christians have embarked upon a race
and a rugged combat. Oil can be used in conjunction with the
laying-on-of-hands, but it should be reserved for its primary sense
of the further chrismating of God's people. Laying-on-of-hands is
for a specific purpose (usually named in the accompanying prayer)
and sometimes administered to people on the fringe of the Church
to bring healing comfort and solace. Anointing with oil is a specific
encounter related to our life in Christ through baptism, as branches
of the one true vine, recalling us ever more closely to our basic
identity in relationship to Christ and our mystical life in him.

STILLNESS AND MOVEMENT: SILENCE AND SPACE

In just the same way as light presupposes shadow and darkness,
so all church furnishings and ceremonial are set within the context
of space. It is so sad to see a church cluttered with pews. There
are few things more telling in church architecture than the nave
of a vast cathedral where the pews have been removed. We see
the pillars then as they were intended to be seen, rising out of
the ground like vast trees, uncluttered and majestic in their isolated
splendor, irresistibly drawing our eyes heavenwards, towards the

larger and more generous environment in which all our earthly activities find their proper proportions. Furniture so often contradicts or even obliterates the basic lines of a building and all that the building is trying to say in its architectural eloquence. How often a church building has come alive for worship when for some practical reason or other it has had to be stripped of all its furnishings. It is not a bad exercise to strip it in the first place and start from scratch. Leave plenty of space for movement. Teach people to come into church and sit or stand in all sorts of parts of the building using the lines and lights of the building as aids to worship. Furthermore, space leaves the opportunity for movement and dance, which are increasingly employed in worship and liturgy today. For ideally the liturgy in itself is a kind of dance with a rhythm of stillness and movement. Each part of the liturgy should naturally flow into the next part without a hiccup of self-consciousness and without any stumbling. Nothing in a well-ordered service need be "given out." Readings should flow into silence and then from there into a vocal response either with an anthem or in the singing of a hymn. Prompting should be kept to the minimum. Where a dance is best used it should heighten and elaborate a movement already integral to the liturgy, like the Gospel or the offertory procession, rather than being an isolated event in itself. Some gospel narratives cry out for some form of part reading (as in the passion narratives) and also for some dance or drama, the more simple, the better. It should never deteriorate into a sophisticated and eclectic activity, for nothing could be further from the hallmark of good liturgy. The stillness and the movement belong to each other and lead us—as in a great symphony or in a ballet—to the natural climax. We should not be ashamed to see good liturgy as an art form requiring all the discipline and skills of other art forms as it creates an interdependence between stillness and movement, silence and speech, symbols and space.

And so to the place of silence in the worship of God. Why is it that we find silence in liturgy so difficult? Of course we all find silence difficult today. Bishop John Baker writes:

Silence can be a terrifying thing. Silence, you see, is quite different
from peace and quiet. You can have peace and quiet over a drink
with friends in a pub, or listening to records with your girl friend,
or using up your energy resources driving out on Sunday. If you
are feeling dreadfully ill, say, with a severe virus infection, but
not delirious, to be left alone in bed, warm and undisturbed, that
is peace and quiet. But suppose you feel all right; suppose you
are in hospital, or in isolation, waiting for the results of crucial
tests, perhaps in a darkened room wanting to know whether your
life can be saved, or immobilized after an eye operation: that is
not peace and quiet, that is silence. And silence is not necessarily
peace.

   Silence is loneliness, perhaps the most acute form of loneliness
there is. If you shut someone in total darkness for long enough,
the brain will invent hallucinations because the absence of visual
stimuli would otherwise drive them mad. In much the same way,
if there is nothing to hear, babel breaks out in our head. Our own
mind starts talking to us, frantically, in a panic. Of course, it says
the first thing that comes into our head, so to speak; but that
may be the very last thing we want to hear.[11]

And there is the clue. Silence in liturgy is not the absence of words
or activity: it is the culmination of words. It heralds the presence
of the Word. Silence is the other side of speech and the natural
fulfilment of it and the climax of all that has gone before it. It is
this understanding of silence that will guide those responsible for
leading worship. There will be nothing awkward or self-conscious
in silence if priests and people alike have learned to be at home
in silence and to respond to it with expectation. Lessons will not
abruptly end with a liturgical guillotine: "The Word of the Lord"
or "Here ends the reading." The words of the lesson will end but
will point us to the presence of the Word in our midst and will
lead us therefore to penitence, thanksgiving, and adoration. There
have been recent experiments with a silent liturgy of the Word.
After the entrance of the priest, the introductory prayers, and an
act of penitence, there is then a period of up to ten or fifteen
minutes of silence in the place where Scripture is usually read.
After this the liturgy continues with the eucharistic prayer. Such

a practice does not arise from any downgrading of the importance of Scripture in worship, but rather from a realization that the power and authority of the written or spoken words of Scripture are derived from the presence and spirit of the silent Word. The words of Scripture are but a "sacrament" of the presence of the hidden and silent Word. All sacraments and Scripture are but vehicles, helping us to receive into our hearts the presence of the Word, so that he may be enfleshed in his people. The Incarnation thus becomes a continuous and contemporary event. "When all things were in quiet silence, and night was in the midst of her swift course, thine all powerful Word leapt down from heaven, out of thy royal throne."[12] Although this is especially the experience of Christians at Christmas, it should also be the joyful experience of all Christians at all times and not least when we are gathered together for worship.

Worship should afford us all kinds of opportunities for silence. What about the silence before the service begins? Why do we always have to have a Prelude, right up to the beginning of the service? It is a pity to think of music being used as a kind of acoustical polyfiller! Perhaps after some music, at about two minutes to time, the simple welcome from the local priest with the announcements and even perhaps a few page numbers as "stage directions" could then be followed by a bidding to silence and expectation. Then at a given (silent please!) signal, the organ bursts out with a play-over of the first hymn and people rise unbidden to their feet for worship and praise. The silence during the service, especially after the solemn reading of God's word, is very important indeed. No one moves—not even the reader—as the last words of the scriptural passage are allowed to ring out with their clarion call to obedience and discipleship. (There is something to be said, sometimes, for no concluding sentence of any kind at this point in the service, as this suggests the termination of the Word, which, as we have said, is not what is happening at all.) There is equally a place for silence after the sermon and certainly at some point in the prayer of the Church. Then there is also the place of stillness—especially for those who are privileged to preside in worship. Stand still! Don't fidget! There should be no pieces of paper or books in your hand, and there should certainly be no cleaning of glasses or fidgeting with handkerchiefs! For God's sake, literally, be still so that you may be a still center for the whole proceedings. (For some clergy this discipline will require a whole course of learning and even a total reordering of their lives; we are, as a race, such inveterate fidgets.)

The hands in worship should be empty: extended, probably raised in prayer before God our Father. The collect should be said strongly and slowly after a bidding and silence, with hands extended and raised (and the book from which it is read should be either held by an attendant or placed on a reading desk). The hands are so important in all worship and the whole people of God should be taught how to use them expressively in their prayer and worship, both private and public.

And finally, the voice. The voice is such an expressive and sensitive instrument of the body. So seldom do clergy know how to use it. Most clergy need to be retrained to discover a good, strong, natural, sensitive voice, pitched neither too high nor too low, too loud nor too soft for the particular occasion. There must be no affectation of any kind. (It is so sad that it is frequently possible to tell from which seminary a man has come the minute he opens his mouth in public worship and in every case it represents a hideous distortion of the good voice God has given him.) The parsonical voice is perhaps only a close second to that most hideous distortion—the hearty voice—with its studied "friendly" and informal note. Worship may be informal, but it is never trivial. There is nothing of the cozy chat about Christian worship; it is an encounter with God who is both our judge and our king as well as our father and our friend. The tone set must be that of taking God seriously, just as we have to take our friends seriously and those whom we love.

So in every way, from the moment of entering the church to the moment of leaving it, everything must conspire to the one end: to bring men and women communally into the presence of God for service, worship, praise, and adoration. It is a massive and skillful undertaking, while at the same time it ultimately depends on the free and unsolicited gift of God's grace and his presence, without which it would degenerate into a meaningless charade. In worship, as in every other area of Christian life, the balance between what we do and what God does for us and in us is not so easy to find. It is perhaps best summed up in the aphorism of St. Augustine: "Without God we cannot; without us he will not."

Nothing less than all of this is the agenda next Sunday morning in every church all across the country as well as in a thousand different cells of Christian worship in homes and in ordinary places where men and women, boys and girls, gather to worship God in Christ. In the lovely words of William Cowper the task for next Sunday morning is powerfully expressed:

> Here may we prove the power of prayer,
> To strengthen faith and sweeten care;
> To teach our faint desires to rise,
> And bring all heaven before our eyes.[13]

7

Receiving the Word of God

THE WORD OF GOD

At the heart of all renewal movements at the present time is an ever-increasing reverence for the word of God in Scripture. Across the whole spectrum of all the churches, and conspicuously in the Roman Catholic Church, the people of God are finding within the Scriptures an authority, power, and presence and are deriving from the reading and study of the Bible a deep and enriching spirituality. Laus Deo! It must also be said, however, that in some areas of renewal this proper reverence for Scripture has unfortunately toppled over into a neo-fundamentalistic approach, and this is both sad and dangerous. There is in mankind, and never very far below the surface, the quest for infallibility in one form or another. It is motivated by that old-fashioned disease we call idolatry and is based upon the misguided conviction that authority and infallibility are necessarily the same thing. In fact, of course, I do not need to be infallible at mathematics in order to be able to speak with authority on prayer, love, marriage, or death. Authority is rooted in experience and is a word that is strongly personal. Infallibility, on the other hand, is more related to data and facts. We need from the outset, therefore, to establish the nature of the authority that is rightly attributed and indeed uniquely attributed by Christians to the Holy Bible before we go on to discuss its use in liturgical worship and in its presentation from the pulpit in preaching and proclamation.

In St. Luke's Gospel, in the story of the resurrection encounter on the road to Emmaus, Jesus shows us how to read the Scriptures by opening them for us and showing us how from "The beginning" through "Moses and all the prophets" all the events are "interpreted" correctly when they are referred to himself, to Jesus, the Word of God made flesh in our midst.[1] The Scriptures point to Jesus because Jesus is the Word of God. Furthermore, the relationship between the Scriptures and the Word of God is a living link which, when we recognize it, enables us to say with the disciples that "our hearts burn within *us*" for we also experience this opening of the Scriptures, the word of God, by Jesus, the Word of God. The authority of Scripture for Christians, therefore, is not rooted in some magical and irrational fundamentalism, but rather in the reality of that living relationship between Jesus, the Word of God made flesh, and the Bible, which is the word and record of God in verbal form. Anterior, therefore, to our understanding of the Bible as the word of God must be our love of Jesus as the Word of God.

"For the word of God is living and active, sharper than any two-edged sword, piercing to the division of soul and spirit, of joints and marrow, and discerning the thoughts and intentions of the heart. And before him no creature is hidden, but all are open and laid bare to the eyes of him with whom we have to do."[2] It is noteworthy that the writer of the epistle to the Hebrews suddenly changes from the word of God as "it" to the word of God as "he." This is because the two are essentially related and both share the same authority. Yet if we go back to the very opening verses of Scripture in the book of Genesis we find that same Word of God in action in creating and forming the universe. "In the beginning God . . . said, let there be light: and there was light." We see God's word enfleshing his will in creation. His word is his deed. His word is not simply some spoken utterance or some written formula: it is his creating power, so that Isaiah in the eighth century before Christ could write of that same word:

For as the rain and the snow come down from heaven, and return
not thither but water the earth, making it bring forth and sprout,
giving seed to the sower and bread to the eater, so shall my word
be that goes forth from my mouth; it shall not return empty, but
it shall accomplish that which I purpose and prosper in the thing
for which I sent it.[3]

So we should not be surprised that for those with eyes to see
and ears to hear the face of this same Jesus is latent in practically
every page of the scriptural record. Rather similar to the leitmotiv
in a Wagnerian opera, the great themes are present, however dimly
and unfully formed, from the earliest records of the Scriptures,
becoming increasingly clear until they are openly orchestrated in
the historical events of the life, death, and resurrection of Jesus
Christ. This process continues in the New Testament, where, by
the work of the Holy Spirit of God, we see the Word of God,
Jesus, formed in the events and lives of the new Israel. "And we
also thank God constantly for this, that when you received the
word of God which you heard from us, you accepted it not as the
word of men but as what it really is, the word of God, which is
at work in you believers."[4] So, when the word of God is preached
or read aloud it must not be viewed as a mere reminiscence but
recognized as a presence. In word and sacrament alike, Christians
know the presence of Jesus and are more conscious of that contemporary presence than of any memory from the past. In Old
Testament prophecy, the Holy Spirit forms the word of God and
points forward to Jesus the Word of God made flesh. In the New
Testament and the subsequent history of the Church, that same
Spirit *represents* the word of God by taking the things of Jesus and
re-presenting them to us.[5] Therefore, the history of revelation is
not so much to be seen chronologically—before and after Christ—as
existentially, as a point of convergence when our "hearts burn within
us," when our "eyes are opened," and when we "recognize" him,
active and present in us. He in turn represents us to the Father[6]
who "recognizes" again his first created word, taking delight in this
further creation as he did at the outset in Genesis when he first
created us and looked upon us with pleasure. So in many ways

we should expect the Bible to be at its most eloquent when it is read formally and unequivocally in the presence of God's people in the course of the liturgy. This is the context in which the words of Scripture take on their fullest meaning, forming and informing God's people week by week with the story of God's revelation of his purposes made evident in the face of Jesus Christ. This being so, it is a grave and onerous responsibility to read the words of Scripture in public worship. For the prime purpose of Scripture is not to stimulate only the intellect or hand on some ideas about God but rather to become truly a part of the Christian.[7] This union is profound, of a sort that inevitably calls for the metaphor of eating. "And he said to me, 'Son of Man, eat what is offered to you; eat this scroll, and go, speak to the house of Israel.' So I opened my mouth, and he gave me the scroll to eat. And he said to me, 'Son of man eat, eat this scroll that I give you and fill your stomach with it.' Then I ate it; and it was in my mouth as sweet as honey."[8] So, in the words of the ancient collect, we are intended to "read, mark, learn and *inwardly digest*" the word of God.[9] Here is the living link between the word of God in the sacrament and the word of God in preaching. Both are in a real sense for the diet and sustenance of the Christian.

Few things are therefore more important when rehearsing and preparing for worship than the careful choice of the right scriptural passages to be read with reverence and expectation. Expectation is that old prophetic question, "Is there a word from the Lord for us?" This should be the expectation, and nothing less, that heralds the reading of Scripture in public worship and its subsequent proclamation in the expounding of that word of God in preaching.

And to read the Scriptures, therefore, is a skill, requiring patience, ability, and a particular charism. In the ancient liturgy of the Church, even a special blessing was bestowed before the reader stood up to read. It is still traditional to this day to bless the deacon before the Gospel is read. It will simply not do to let any member of the laity, on a democratic basis, read the lessons in church. As much care and consideration (if not more) should be given to this activity in the liturgy as is given to authorizing the laity to give the cup at communion. Furthermore, it should be undertaken in such a way that it shows from the outset the important place the Scriptures have in living worship. There must be no informal walking to the lectern carrying a scrappy copy of the service on which the passage from Scripture is written. The Bible should be carried into the church formally and solemnly (preferably by the deacon) at the outset of the service and held high in the opening procession. Placed on the holy table, it is then taken formally and solemnly to the place in the building from which it is to be read. It is the holy Bible and we must make this clear and explicit in our every action.

In passing, it may not be inappropriate to comment upon a new habit that has been introduced in many churches of reading a short passage of explanation before the passage of Scripture is read. May it be suggested that this really overlaps with another valid—but rather different—exercise and that this exercise is not appropriate to Christian worship? Of course there is a place for commentaries and of course there is a place for some kind of summary of a passage of Scripture. But the word of God in formal worship must be allowed to speak for itself or to be formally expounded in the sermon or homily. It is not right to superimpose upon it from the outset just one, partially valid, expression of its power and force. Spoken clearly and read well, the words of Scripture have the power to convert as powerfully as they had when St. Anthony of Egypt first heard the call of Jesus to leave all and was ready to obey that call immediately, with the simplicity and immediacy the words of Scripture demanded as they were solemnly read at mass for the Gospel of the day. Can you imagine anything more calculated to rob those challenging demands of Jesus of their power and authority than some well-intentioned and soft-edged "explanation"? The Scriptures do not primarily call to be explained. They demand first, and before all else, to be obeyed.

"Read, mark, learn and inwardly digest." We need as God's people to know whole passages of the Scripture by heart just as Jesus himself knew the words of Scripture. Three of the seven words from the cross are words of Scripture, regurgitated as "comfortable words" when ordinary words and articulation were no longer possible. So then, we must ask seriously about the multiplicity of translations used in worship today. Perfectly good though these may be on the study shelves for reference, in Bible study groups or in private study of the Scriptures, they cannot nevertheless provide the staple diet of God's people. Sooner, rather than later, we need to settle on one basic translation that can be the agreed text of the people of God and become increasingly known by heart by a churchgoing generation that is (strangely enough in an age of reading) almost scripturally illiterate. *Embarras de choix* is all right in a supermarket, but it has robbed a whole generation of churchgoing Christians of a basic part of their diet: that inward digestion of well-read, well-marked, and well-learned Scripture.

Such must be the priority given to the reading of Scriptures in the liturgy of the Church that, when the passage of Scripture is finished, if there is to be silence for a while (and probably in most cases there should be), then there is no need for a concluding sentence, whether it be "The word of the Lord" or "Here ends the reading." Such phrases have the effect of cutting off that section of the service. Rather, as the last sentence of the words of the lesson die away, let the reader remain standing for a period of silence—a silence only broken by the playing over of the hymn or an unannounced anthem or motet from the choir reflecting upon the previous word of Scripture. (It is especially important at this point not to lapse suddenly into giving out hymn numbers or stage directions.) The reading should lead naturally into recollection and the recollection should lead naturally into a response in song, prayer, or praise.

OPENING THE SCRIPTURES

"Then he opened their minds to understand the scriptures, and said to them, "Thus it is written, that the Christ should suffer and on the third day rise from the dead, and that repentance and forgiveness of sins should be preached in his name to all nations,

beginning from Jerusalem. You are witnesses to these things.' "[10]
Incapsulated in that text is the basis of all Christian teaching and
preaching for it has the authority of the risen Christ and shows
us the model of apostolic preaching commissioned directly by the
risen Christ. There are two aspects to preaching: "the opening of
the minds" to the record of Scripture and the validating of what
is heard in the insight and experience of those who are listening
who are intended to be "witnesses." So once again, at every moment
and at every turn, we see the Word being made flesh—enfleshed—
in the lives of those who hear and receive this word of God. The
Word of God forms the people of God, so when Karl Barth was
asked how he prepared his Sunday sermon, he replied: "I take the
Bible in one hand and the newspaper in the other." The Incarnation
is therefore a continuing process: Jesus, the Word, is received by
and enfleshed in his people by word and sacrament so that they
in their turn become the people of God to be witnesses of his death
and resurrection. All this is through the work and overshadowing
of the Holy Spirit, as it was at the outset when the word was made
flesh at the Annunciation. And the end product is always the same:
to form the Word of God who dwells richly in the hearts of those
who receive him. We are all in that sense intended to be *theotokoi*
(God bearers) as was Mary, the mother of the Lord. It is the activity
of the Holy Spirit to re-present Jesus and to make him present
at all times and in all places for his people by the breaking open
of the Word and by the breaking of bread. When Christian preaching takes place, as St. Augustine is at pains to point out, God
himself is present in it. When God's word is "preached and in as
much as the preacher speaks the truth, Christ speaks through
him."[11] With such a high doctrine you might well ask, "Who is
equal to these things?" The answer must reside in our doctrine
of preaching. No one achieves the gift of preaching, for, like all
gifts in the New Testament, it is not achieved but rather received.
It is a mighty commission. Nevertheless, the most important thing
will be that we know what we are doing before we seek to know
how to do it. It is perhaps in the realm of the doctrine of preaching that the Church in recent decades has lost its nerve most

conspicuously, so there can be no doubt that we need to recover our doctrine in this field if we are to recover our confidence as preachers. For supremely, preaching is the activity of God. It is an event and not simply an essay or an exercise. Perhaps that is the reason why a sermon which moved us and was so formative in our Christian discipleship is frequently rather a disappointment and even a letdown when we subsequently read it. A large part of its power belonged to the event and is not contained in a visual representation of the words in the script. Something *happens* when the word of God is preached among the people of God. But does it?

What happens does not have to be spectacular—though it frequently has been in the history of the Church, changing people's lives dramatically. Nor does it have to be memorable—though it frequently has been in the lives of those who often recall it until the end of their days. But it does have to be substantial and authentic and part of a regular and balanced diet so that God's people may be reguarly fed and built up and sustained. "Sermonettes make christianettes!" There can be no doubt that there will be no lasting renewal in worship unless there is a real renewal in our expectation about preaching, both by the preacher and by those who receive God's word through his ministry. St. Augustine saw preaching essentially as feeding the Lord's people and the pulpit as "the Lord's table, at which the minister ought not to defraud his guests."[12] He sees the Christian congregation assembled for nothing less than a banquet in which the preacher has the responsibility of feeding the guests until they are satisfied. It is not true that sermons are boring or that the spoken word is no longer effective. Bad preaching will always be boring and certainly will not be effective, but there will never be a church in which there is not a place for preaching. Furthermore, there is no doctrine in the New Testament that teaches that sermons have to last only twenty minutes! It has to be admitted, though, that in a highly competitive world of words the preacher must have skill as well as sincerity if he is to arrest our attention. Where there is a living preacher there is a living Church and that fact alone lays upon both the ordained ministry as well as upon other ministries in the Church a heavy and costly

responsibility. "Here is the miracle of the divine economy," writes
Donald Coggan, "that between the forgiveness of God and the sin
of man stands—*the preacher!* That between the provision of God
and the need of man stands—*the preacher!* It is his task to link
human sin to forgiveness, human need to divine omnipotence,
human search to divine revelation."[13]

For preaching is not quite like anything else on earth. It is not
the same as teaching, a lecture, an essay, or an oration; yet it clearly
overlaps with all of these categories of communication. In many
ways it is most like an old-fashioned music hall. Preacher and
congregation are both participating and both get caught up in this
great event. The congregation should participate to such an extent
that the preacher will see people's faces changing before his very
eyes, maybe with anger, puzzlement, or indifference, or they may
nod (hopefully not just because they are falling asleep) as the "penny
is dropping" and the preacher is making a telling point that rings
true in the experience, the hearts and lives of those who are listening. In St. Augustine's day, the congregation would frequently
applaud in the basilica and sometimes would show other responses,
either of appreciation or the opposite. All of this we see in book
four of his "De Doctrina Christiana," where the bishop of Hippo
describes his daily experience of expounding the word of God,
generally seated on his cathedra (chair) in his basilica at Hippo.
Augustine was a preaching man from start to finish who had given
his life over to the study of Scripture and to the expounding of
it. Augustine, like St. Paul before him, spoke of preaching as the
paying of a debt.[14] "Preach wherever you can, to whom you can
and as you can."[15] It is indeed a lifetime's craft and a daily burden
and responsibility.

What is increasingly clear in the renewal of the contemporary
Church is that a written sermon in a detached style, which is
distinctive and reminiscent of an art form of an earlier age, will
simply no longer fit the bill. There was a time when worship was
institutionalized and the sermon in its own turn became an institutionalized art form. Read and study the great nineteenth-century
preachers, value them and applaud them, but do not seek to copy

them. Today, preaching is best learned on the small occasion, a house Eucharist, or even a low mass when the lectionary of the day provides the bread which demands to be taken by the preacher and broken open in the presence of the people of God. Thus, there appears to be something much more spontaneous about preaching today. Yet make no mistake about it, all preaching (great or small) requires preparation. The question is, where and how? More and more remote preparation, less and less immediate preparation. For the "preaching man" should carry around with him day in and day out the burden of his message, requiring daily and detailed study of the Scriptures and an alert and sensitive mind tuned to the casual remark during visiting, a line from a poster, an advertisement or a song, a newspaper article, a television series, or just "the words of the prophets . . . written on the subway walls."[16] John Stott in his excellent book on preaching tells how he studies four chapters of Scripture every day to enable him to read the whole of the Scriptures in the course of one year—the Old Testament once and the New Testament twice.[17] That is the preparation for which there is no substitute. Of course, the secret of preaching is not just in the words (however appropriate). St. Augustine is swift to remind us that:

> the sound of our words strikes the ear, but the master is within. You must not think that anyone learns from the man. The noise of our voice can be no more than a prompting; if there is no teacher within, that noise of ours is useless. . . . [O]utward teachings are but a kind of help and prompting: the teacher of hearts has his chair in heaven.[18]

Nevertheless, there is no substitute for the daily study of the Scriptures as the background of all our preaching. This is the raw material of a lifetime's desire to expound the word of God.

The trigger point of the sermon is the word of Scripture. The word becomes flesh again by the activity of the Holy Spirit; we find Christ truly in our midst in the contemporary applications of the Scriptures just as surely as he is present when bread is broken and wine is outpoured. What thus appears spontaneous is part of a

known process with a theological explanation. The preacher is free
to stand or sit, to look at his hearers, to be flexible to the needs
of the moment, to relate to his congregation and to change his
tactics at any point if someone is looking bored, if anyone has to
leave because they are suddenly not well or if a child starts to cry.
Augustine counsels us to look out for signs of weariness in the
congregation (there really is nothing new under the sun anywhere!)
and challenges the preacher to respond to this,

> by saying something seasoned with discreet cheerfulness, and
> suited to the matter in hand, or something very wonderful and
> amusing, or it may be, something painful and mournful; and such
> as may affect himself rather than another, in order that being
> pinched by concern for self he may continue to be watchful.[19]

In all this a living relationship strikes up between the preacher
and those who are listening: "One loving heart sets another on fire."
This cannot be done in a stylized setting with a well-turned and
stylized script. Augustine, who was the professional orator and
rhetorician of his day, trained in the art of speaking in the ancient
world, nevertheless cautions the preacher that all these models
must be thrown to the winds for this one sacred and unique vocation
of preaching God's word. It really is like nothing else on earth.
So he could remind himself, as well as others, "What matters it
to us, what the grammarians please to rule? It were better for us
to be guilty of a barbarism so that you understand than that in
propriety of speech you are left unprovided."[20]

Of course there is always a place in preaching for the illustration,
but the illustrations must always be pertinent, realistic, vivid, and
easily at hand. They must not be forced, calculated, or self-conscious. Augustine's preaching is brimful of basic stories and illustrations that have about them an authenticity. These homely
illustrations stand, as parables do, as good stories in themselves,
proclaiming the truth without too much help from the preacher's
purple pencil.

In his handbook on Christian preaching, Augustine is not
ashamed to admit he was in the persuading business: "A preacher

is not a salesman. It is his duty to persuade, but not necessarily to please."[21] Augustine writes, "To teach is a necessity, to please is a sweetness, but to persuade is a victory."[22] That victory is sadly lacking in so much preaching today. Men and women should not leave worship the same as they entered it. The task and glorious responsibility of the preacher is to convince and to convert. He slowly moves God's pilgrim people along the king's highway, making sure (by loving persuasion, by skill, by word, and by power of speech) that they have not settled down at some "tavern" on the roadside, moved in, put up the drapes, pulled down the shutters, and put up their feet! Each year, for God's pilgrim people, is a year of grace, marking movement and growth, and much of this can only be achieved by regular feeding through God's word, ministered faithfully and skillfully, week by week, under the power and direction of God's Holy Spirit.

We might well ask what the right subject matter is for preaching. "It (the sermon) need not be eloquent, but it must be about God and have within it the awareness of this presence."[23] It is still a useful discipline for most preachers most of the time to take a text and to expound it. Preaching must be biblical, but that is not the same as saying that the preacher will only preach about the Bible. "A sermon needs to be expressed in the great thought forms of the Scriptures as well as using their content. It is the interpretation of the scriptural point of view, not simply, as it were, quotations from the book."[24] We might also go on today to ask whether there is a place for politics from the pulpit. Of course it depends on what you mean. Bishop Terwilliger, himself conspicuous as a distinguished preacher in the Anglican communion, puts it most succinctly: "The preacher has no right to use his apostolic authority outside the apostolic realm. That is to say, he is not ordained to preach economics or politics, but he is ordained to declare the relationship between the word of God and the ways of man."[25] St. Paul puts it perhaps even more succinctly with the caution: "Woe to me if I do not preach the gospel!"

The outworkings of the sermon are of course very important through Bible-study groups, house groups, and prayer groups. No

one would pretend that all the teaching ministry in a parish can
or should be done through sermons, but it is a huge misconception
that groups can be a total substitute for the spoken proclamation
of the word through a sermon or homily in the context of worship.
For in many ways the only suitable culmination of a sermon is
worship itself. Education (as we see in the story of the wise men)
is a pilgrimage or journey of exploration culminating in worship.
When men and women have been persuaded by the power of the
spoken word they need to move straight into repentance, worship,
or adoration: "My Lord and my God." This is especially true in
mission services. There must be such a shape to mission services
that the sermon points beyond itself to further worship, deeper
praise and adoration, or a new commitment of heart and will. Indeed, there should be in all preaching, as there is in the Eucharist,
a real *anaphora*—a lifting-up of the hearts of the hearers. The
culmination of a sermon is the realization that the Word is present.
Then there is only one thing to do—shut up! Silence is the right
response and worship the proper posture when a sermon has
reached its point, as surely as worship and the release of gifts
marked the goal of all the journeyings of those wise men in search
of their king. Edward King, bishop of Lincoln, used to say that
the shape of a sermon was more or less the shape of a traditional
church building: entrance and introduction; a central theme (the
nave) with illustrations on the side as you went along (the aisles).
But it must lead men and women into the sanctuary and the presence and awareness of the holy. It is not, in other words, simply
enough to inform, entertain, or even educate—though all that is
part of the task of the preacher. In the end, apostolic preaching
must really and truly move people into a closer and deeper awareness of the presence of the Word made flesh, Jesus Christ their
Lord and Savior. So in a Eucharist, the sermon or homily can
inform and direct the time of prayer that generally follows it or,
equally, lead straight into Christian affirmation of the words of the
creed. In other services, it is good to lead from preaching into
silence or a hymn, sung kneeling (perhaps before the blessed sacrament) or just into the reflective singing of choruses of Scripture,

seated still and open to the sweet and blessed influence of God's presence in his Word. Above all, the sermon should not be just another thing put into the service: "Is there to be a sermon today?" The sermon flows inevitably out of the reading of Scripture and flows freely into prayer, affirmation, confession, and adoration. It is an integral part of the movement of all worship.

The renewal of the Church today will draw much of its power from the word of God in Scripture and in preaching as surely as it did in earlier chapters of renewal throughout history. Speaking of the reformation movement, E.C. Dargan comments:

> The great events and achievements of that mighty revolution were largely the work of preachers and preaching; for it was by the word of God, through the ministry of earnest men who believed, loved and taught it, that the best and most enduring work of the Reformation was done. And, conversely, the events and principles of the movement powerfully reacted on preaching itself, giving it new spirit, new power, new forms, so that the relation between the Reformation and preaching may be succinctly described as one of mutual dependence, aid and guidance.[26]

This could be said of all movements of renewal in the history of the Church and equally so of the contemporary movements of renewal in the Church today. Nevertheless, we need to end where we began, with the realization that the first victory is the basic doctrinal conviction about the primacy and priority of God's word in the life of God's people. It was perhaps that basic conviction that had slipped so far in the conventional Church at the beginning of this century; and it is the recovery of that conviction, accompanied by great and vigorous expectations, that is uppermost in the work of renewal today. "To me the work of preaching," writes Dr. Martyn Lloyd-Jones, "is the highest and the greatest and the most glorious calling to which anyone can ever be called. If you want something in addition to that I would say without any hesitation that the most urgent need in the Christian Church today is true preaching."[27] Or, from a very different source—the second

Vatican Council—the preacher and the priest are exhorted with the words:

> Since no one can be saved who had not first believed, priests, as co-workers with their bishops, have as their primary duty the proclamation of the gospel of God to all. . . . The task of priests is not to teach their own wisdom but God's word, and to summon all men urgently to conversion and to holiness. . . . Such preaching does not present God's word in a general abstract fashion only, but it must apply the perennial truth of the gospel to the concrete circumstances of life.[28]

Worship, Service, and Life

WORSHIP INCLUDES ALL LIFE and the moments spent in concentrated worship, whether in church or elsewhere, are the focusing points of the sustaining and directing energy of the worshipper's whole life."[1]

We saw from the outset that true worship is a whole way of seeing God's world from God's point of view in Christ. Although true worship transcends the world, it does not bypass it and so in that sense Archbishop Temple in the quotation above is right: "Worship *includes* all life." The mandate of the Eucharist is nothing less than a vision in which the worshipper sees "heaven and earth" as "full of his glory." For those with eyes to see and ears to hear that is the texture of the universe.

But this vision is not disclosed automatically. Christian worship begins with what is natural and then moves on to the supernatural. It starts with bread but ends with body. It starts with wine and ends with a life-giving transfusion of blood. Because of the incarnation of Christ, the dynamic of Christian worship begins with the supernatural plunging into the earth and into the natural. Because of the ascension of Christ, worship is completed by raising the natural into the fuller and further environment of heaven and the supernatural. Yet this must be seen as one whole dynamic and as the overall perspective of God's purposes for the universe. So the record of Scripture is right: "In saying, 'he ascended,' what does it mean but that he also descended into the lower parts of the earth? He who descended is he who also ascended far above all the heavens, that he might fill all things."[2] So in Christian worship there should be no fragmentation, nor rejection of some parts of life as merely secular or profane. This was the supreme lesson Peter had to learn in his vision at Joppa[3]: the old schizophrenic distinctions between things "profane" in themselves and things "sacred" in themselves—that ancient dilemma for God's people—had finally been abolished in Christ. Indeed, perhaps it is possible to hazard a distinction between Christian worship and other comparable transcendental experiences by demanding that in Christian worship we *gather up* the fragments that remain in order that nothing may be lost.[4] Worship must lead to holiness, which is the very opposite of fragmentation. Aldous Huxley makes this point most eloquently when he comments on his own transcendental experiences after taking the drug mescalin. Something analogous to contemplation is clearly happening, but it is a contemplation and a transcendental experience very remote from the Christian understanding of worship. He writes:

> But now I knew contemplation at its height. At its height, but not yet in its fullness. For in its fullness, the way of Mary, includes the way of Martha and raises it, so to speak, to its own higher power. Mescalin opens up the way of Mary, but shuts the door on that of Martha. It gives access to contemplation—but to a contemplation that is incompatible with action and even with the will to action.[5]

Christian worship has always set its face against this kind of fragmentation and regarded it as blatant escapism. A contemplation "incompatible with action" is not Christian contemplation, for the claim of Christian worship has always been *orare est laborare: laborare est orare*. Each belongs to the other and each is rooted firmly within the other so that in the end "nothing is lost." Indeed, in the language of the Jews, the word for worship is a derivation from the root, *abad*, which basically means to serve. There is in Jewish and Christian tradition alike, therefore, no antithesis between the worship of God and the service of the community. Worship and service are one. So William Temple can again write: "All life ought to be worship; and we know quite well that there is no chance that it will be worship unless we have times when we have worship and nothing else."[6] Once again he is affirming the principle we have discovered earlier in the book: the route to the universal is through the way of the particular. We need specific moments of worship in order to insure that life at all moments can be offered as worship. So he can boldly and confidently continue: "Our duty to God requires that we should, for a good part of our time, be not consciously thinking about him. That makes it absolutely necessary . . . that we should have our times which are worship, pure and simple."[7] It is from these moments of "pure and simple worship" that we emerge as "God's spies" *(King Lear)* with vision equipped to explore and discover that heaven and earth are indeed full of his glory.

Seen in this way, there can be no dichotomy between the gospel of the sanctuary and the gospel of social concern: when the worship is ended the service truly begins! So once again, Temple summarizes this single vision of one world. "If then the Christian citizen is to make his Christianity tell upon his politics, his business, his social enterprises, he must be a churchman—consciously belonging to the worshipping fellowship and sharing its worship—before he is a citizen; he must bring the concerns of his citizenship and his business before God and go forth to them carrying God's inspiration with him."[8] There is, for a Christian, therefore, no hard line between the secular and the sacred—unfortunately! It would be so much more convenient if there were, because the secular could then belong to a separate compartment of life, free from any possibility of invasion from the sacred. The secular is plunged into the sacred (as in the Eucharist at the offertory) to become the Body of Christ, but precisely in order that in turn the sacred may be let loose on the unsuspecting world of the secular in a million and one indirect, subtle, and mysterious ways through the agency of the other body of Christ—the Christian, undermining society at its very roots, yet largely unobserved except by those with eyes to see. This kind of vision, however, makes all the difference in the world because it makes a social gospel inevitable without permitting it to deteriorate into patronizing concern; it generates an evangelism that is effective without being self-conscious and rescues stewardship and any concern for environmentalism from legalism and pusillanimous phariseeism.

WORSHIP AND THE SOCIAL GOSPEL

The motivation of the social gospel cannot simply be love of our neighbor. We do not go to others from our strength to their weakness; such a view of care and concern will all too easily degenerate into patronizing and do-gooding. Here, as elsewhere, we need a vision that compels us to go where we would not choose to go, to love those whom we would not choose to love, and to share with others whom we would not choose as friends. So in the gospel we have the vision that brings to service and care a single and powerful motivation: "I say to you, as you did it to one of the least of these my brethren, you did it to me."[9] It is the same Jesus whom we worship and serve and recognize by faith in the bread and wine at the Eucharist whom we worship, serve, and recognize by faith in the homeless, the hungry, the sick, and the imprisoned. Only if we *recognize* him here in these places will he *recognize* us before the Father. It is that "recognition" from both sides that brings authenticity to worship and service, both in the sanctuary as well as in the slums. In a single statement, Jesus rescues all our concern for others from anything that could remotely be called patronizing, by focusing worship and service alike on the mystery of the Incarnation: Jesus hidden in the bread and wine, in matter and in every atom, but that same Jesus also hidden in the face of every person in need, poverty, or sickness. So we simply cannot have the one without the other and in either case to fail to "recognize" Jesus is to commit that most serious of offenses so terrifyingly cautioned by St. Paul of "failing to discern the body."[10] We shall not come to know the full catholic Christ until we learn

to recognize him both within what he refuses to call secular, as
well as in what we choose to call sacred. He is the Lord of both
alike. So St. John Chrysostom can write:

> Would you honor the body of Christ? Do not despise his naked-
> ness; do not honor him here in church clothed in silk vestments
> and then pass him by unclothed and frozen outside. Remember
> that he who said, "This is my Body," and make good his words,
> also said, "You saw me hungry and gave me no food," and "in
> so far as you did it not to one of these, you did it not to me."
> In the first sense the body of Christ does not need clothing but
> worship from a pure heart. In the second sense it does need
> clothing and all the care we can give it. We must learn to be
> discerning Christians and to honor Christ in the way in which
> he wants to be honored. I am not saying you should not give
> golden altar vessels and so on, but I am insisting that nothing
> can take the place of almsgiving. What is the use of loading Christ's
> table with gold cups while he himself is starving? Will you make
> a cup of gold, and withhold a cup of water? What use is it to adorn
> the altar with cloth of gold hangings and deny Christ a coat for
> his back? What would that profit you? Consider that Christ is that
> tramp who comes in need of a night's lodging. You turn him away
> and then start laying rugs on the floor, draping the walls, hanging
> lamps on silver chains on the columns. Adorn the house of God
> if you will, but do not forget your brother in distress. He is a
> temple of infinitely greater value.[11]

So there should be no fear that by placing concern for well-
ordered worship high on the list of our priorities as a Church we
are turning away from the concerns of the inner city, the Third
World, or the social gospel. On the contrary, perhaps we should
expect that men's hearts will grow faint and love will grow cold
in these very areas unless the Church seeks also to bring the vision
of true worship onto the agenda of social welfare. There have been
conspicuous chapters in the life of the Church when beautiful worship and compassionate service have belonged to the same agenda,
could be found within the same streets, and were notoriously
contesting for first place at the top of the list of the priorities of

the Church. The Christian socialist movement in the late nineteenth century in England was much inspired by what we would call "high-church" worship, while the Clapham Sect was equally influenced by strong evangelical preaching for conversion. It is Christ who gave to high-church worship and evangelical preaching alike a common concern for the poor and the needy. It was a later distortion of the gospel to see it and the social gospel as alternatives or opposites or, worse still, as options we can choose according to our inclinations.

For perhaps it has to be admitted that only where there is a high doctrine of Jesus and his presence (whether catholic or evangelical) is there a really compassionate vocation to serve the world. Unitarians have not in general been conspicuous for a social gospel; and wherever worship is merely an edifying and pleasant aesthetic experience, then historically the Church has tended to retreat into indifference to social ills, political commitment, and social justice. In a very telling passage from *Christian Faith and Life*, William Temple points with subtlety to this very issue:

> When we have been absorbed in great music, I do not think we generally feel particularly charitable to the people we meet outside. They seem to be of a coarser fiber than that into which we have been entering. That could never be true of our worship if it has really been worship of God, not some indulgence of our own spiritual emotion, but the concentration of mind, heart and will on him. You will be full of kindness for everybody as you go out from such worship.[12]

Jesus redeems our worship from being just a pleasant aesthetic indulgence by reminding us from start to finish that it was only by his incarnation that the doors of heaven could ever be open to flesh and blood at all.

Therefore, if we are going to sail on the ticket of his incarnation, we soon discover to our cost that it is not a one-way ticket from earth to heaven (a get-away-from-it-all on a long weekend!) but rather what is commonly called "a round-trip" from heaven to earth and all the way back again, via a stable door, Gethsemane, and

Calvary hill. To end up at his right hand or his left hand will almost certainly involve being on his right hand or his left next to that other throne—a bloody cross on Calvary hill. These are not alternatives. They are both centers of a single love and therefore of a single worship, adoration, and service.

WORSHIP AND EVANGELISM

There is another false polarization of alternatives that does not exist in reality: concern for worship over and against evangelism; kneeling in the sanctuary or standing on the soap box. The very first apostolic miracle recorded in the book of the Acts of the Apostles recounts how the healed man who had been lame entered the temple with Peter and John "walking and leaping and praising God." It goes on to record that when "all the people saw him walking and praising God" they in their turn were "filled with wonder and amazement."[13] St. Luke shows that this complex of events is a constant theme in the healing miracles: healing and release expressed in worship, with the spin-off of witness and evangelism to others who are standing by and observing the power of that release expressed so vividly in worship. So in St. Luke's account of the healing of the blind man we are specifically told that, as soon as he received his sight, he followed Jesus "glorifying God" and then—almost as an incidental result yet clearly concomitant with that release and worship—we are told explicitly that "all the people, when they saw it, gave praise to God."[14] Notice, there is nothing self-conscious about the evangelistic spin-off; the healing and worship were not offered for an evangelistic purpose. Far from it. In fact, Jesus is careful in the New Testament to reject the form of evangelism that relies upon spectacular events in order to promote faith. The release and worship are ends in themselves. Nevertheless, they carry with them the almost inevitable result of reaching out to others, causing them either to follow suit or at least to go away asking themselves the right sort of questions.

So, authentic worship is not an alternative to evangelism; on the contrary, it is a necessary and prior ingredient in the total process, laying the foundations for persuasive evangelism. To say this does not suppose, however, that we should regard the Church's worship as primarily for the sake of the newcomer, the enquirer, or the "man in the street." The worship of the Church is not intended to take place in the shop window of the Church, commending the goods that are on sale. There was an unfortunate chapter in the history of the Church when we thought that worship had to be made "understandable" for the sake of the enquirer who might be present for the first time. Not only is this not really practical, it is totally undesirable. In the early Church it was not possible for the neophyte (the new Christian) to attend the full Eucharist until he had been baptized and confirmed. Furthermore, the catechumen could only attend worship if he was already receiving instruction. In the present world, and in western society at least, Sunday morning worship is increasingly for the initiated. It is unlikely that there will be pews of people who are there for the first time or who have dropped in casually for one of their occasional visits.

Nevertheless, men and women released into authentic worship will be vehicles of God's love and their lives will speak of the power and the presence of the God they have come to know and love in worship. Furthermore, we can see how evangelists will, rightly though dangerously, use powerful and authentic worship to release people into deeper and more committed discipleship. In evangelistic services there is a real place for singing and adoration, praying and praising; for the creation of an environment in which the mind is stilled *within* the heart, the affections, and emotions, and in which deeper faith is elicited through the powerful preaching of the word culminating in an act of worship and rededication. Worship and the word should conspire together to convince and convert. There can be no doubt that it is to churches where worship and the word are presented with authenticity and care that people go. You will not find a full church where worship is badly done, and you will soon find a fuller church where it is well done and where the word is preached with power. The conclusion is unavoidable. Worship and evangelism belong together and always have belonged together since the days of the first apostolic preaching.

WORSHIP AND STEWARDSHIP

If we need to rescue evangelism from its isolation from worship, we equally need, especially in the Anglican Church, to rescue stewardship from becoming just a thing in itself, a special department in ecclesiastical life.

Of course, it is incontrovertible that in the Bible and not least in the parables of Jesus there is a strong and recurring theme which sees man as being called to exercise a responsible stewardship in the use of the world, his environment, the universe, and all its resources. But in the Bible there is so much imagery; no one image is sufficient to tell the whole tale of God's purposes for man and his world. We are deliberately confronted with a consortium of apparently conflicting images, for this is the only way we can be rescued from idolatry. If we set up stewardship as the overriding image of man's relationship to his environment, we shall end up with a rather mean, legalistic, and even pharisaical view of man's responsibility within the universe. Something at the present moment about the environmentalists takes us within a hair's breadth of that most dangerous kind of religion: religion obsessed with the cleaning of the outside of the cup at the expense of the cleaning of the inside.[15] So, alongside this image of stewardship, we must also look carefully at the apparently conflicting image of the *prodigality* of God, which runs throughout the whole of the Scriptures. There is an aspect of God that is incredibly wasteful: He is a God who is far too generous by half, for whom the waterpots must be filled and filled to the brim[16] and with whom the grain is always pressed down and running over.[17] Man is perhaps most godlike when he is also most generous in going that "second mile" beyond the first[18] required by law, in giving his cloak as well as his coat.[19]

So it is with worship. In Christian worship, the offering of ourselves is part of our act of thanksgiving and Eucharist. The woman with the alabaster jar of costly ointment, therefore, is integral to any recounting of the gospel. Indeed, we are specifically told that wherever the gospel is recorded, this story within the gospel must not be forgotten. Her love of Jesus led her in her generosity to waste something that could in fact have been sold and the money so raised could have been given to the poor. Yet it was a traitor and a thief who argued that case. Worship is the vehicle that carries us beyond our cautious selves and inevitably bids us break the limits of mathematical calculation with an overriding generosity inspired by an overwhelming thankfulness.

Stewardship, the giving of money, the free, unsolicited offering of precious objects to the Church, has been an embarrassment for the Church throughout its history. For wherever Jesus has been most conspicuously present in worship, the problem is always what to do with all the money and the gifts showered upon the Church from thankful, praising, and prayerful hearts. The rot set in (if you will forgive the phrase) with David in the Old Testament! He was thankful to God for deliverance and wanted to set up an altar of thanksgiving to express his gratitude. Someone was foolish enough to offer him a free "threshing floor" for the purpose. David in a moment of prodigality and enthusiasm replied: "I will not offer to the Lord that which costs me nothing."[20] So from David—hardly the most cautious of stewards—to the woman with the alabaster jar of costly ointment and right through the subsequent history of the Church, we see how worship releases an overwhelming generosity and gratitude.

A worshipping Church, therefore, will never be a poor Church. It is significant that in the Prayer Book of Cranmer, the only place in worship where a collection was mandatory was, in fact, the Eucharist, precisely because that is essentially the right setting for the offering of our money—essentially within the framework of thanksgiving. Furthermore, such offering is made because it should reflect the one great costly offering of love made to the Father by the Son and reciprocally within the life of the blessed Trinity. Wherever men and women have been released into that kind of love through the worship of God, they have opened their hearts, their purses, and their pocketbooks and the Church has never been poor. Its greatest, lasting, and only problem has been what to do with all its riches. In living Churches of word and worship there are no financial problems today and there never will be till the close of the age. "Love so amazing, so divine, demands my soul, my life, my all."[21]

So all this talk of percentages in giving to the Church is a man-made distortion of what Christians should really mean by alms-giving. It is true, of course, that in the Old Testament you were required to tithe. This was because of the logic and law of the synagogue. A synagogue required a minimum quorum of ten men and it did not require a mathematical expert to realize that ten men contributing a tenth of their income would constitute a living and financially viable synagogue, able to support a rabbi who would receive a living salary. But that is the old law. Christians live by grace and once you begin to think in those terms you certainly do not get what you deserve—thank God! Grace is not earned or given out fairly. Grace is literally "amazing" in its abundance. Christians do not need and are not required to give a tenth or a twentieth or any other percentage of their income. It could be said that they are not required to give anything at all—yet it could equally well be said that they are expected to give everything and still know that they are "unprofitable" servants.[22] This must be the mark of Christian generosity, and will only arise from a worshipping and thankful heart. There will always be plenty to pay bills and plenty left over to give away, if grace and nothing less than grace is the measure of our giving, and thankful worship is the context in which all our transactions are undertaken.

9

"With Angels and Archangels and with All the Company of Heaven"

THE NUTS AND BOLTS OF RENEWAL IN WORSHIP, such as we have been discussing in previous chapters, are intended for no lesser end than the discovery within sinful, yet redeemed humanity, of the capacity for eternity. For true worship is a "passage" *(pascha)* from time into eternity, from the Church into the kingdom. Christian worship begins on the earth but ends in the heavens; it begins in the mossy and damp warmth of earth, but its goal is the fresh air and bracing environment of the kingdom. What we taste, celebrate, and experience even now, as the Church in time, is already realized and fulfilled by the Church in heaven. "Lift up your hearts." And the response? The original response in the early Church would be better translated: "They are already with the Lord." So in that sense we simply cannot and dare not speak of the worship of the Church as being simply down to earth. It is sad that it takes the man in the street to remind the jaded professionals that an act of worship has "moved" him. So it should, but in a fuller sense than the man in the street so often means. In a full theological appreciation of worship, the worshipper enters into Christ's own *pascha,* passover. He is literally moved over in that passage and is carried with all that he is and all that he has into what is rightly called his inheritance—the kingdom of light. So although there is a renewal in worship in the Churches at the present time, alongside that renewal there is also a liturgical crisis, because in many places so much of the worship we experience is neither one thing nor the other. It has either got stuck in a cerebral reductionism where it is colorless and meaningless (precisely because it set out to be so meaningful!), or it is fixed in a cult of worship that experiences worship only as "a departure out of the world for a little while, as a 'vent' or break in earthly existence, opened up for the inlet of grace."[1]

There are at least three main reasons for this. Sadly, at least among western Christians, there has occurred an almost total disconnection between the study of liturgy and the other theological disciplines. This has resulted in the distortion of what should be a single and seamless robe of reality. Theology—again largely in the west and persistently in the English school—has tended to concentrate on the Scriptures and on biblical criticism, leaving the study of liturgy to degenerate into a largely historical (if not archeological) research into ecclesiastical rubrics. This has brought about a strange state of affairs in both camps. For theology that tends to be derived almost exclusively from scriptural and (even worse) from merely textural criticism rapidly degenerates in its turn into a kind of inverted scriptural fundamentalism. In fact, there is ever-increasing evidence that the Scriptures themselves were formulated within a strongly liturgical context. It would seem not only that large portions of Scripture were already part of the liturgy as hymns and prayers within the New Testament period, but furthermore, much of the "scoring" of the New Testament was in a liturgically orchestrated context.

The issue does not end there. For we cannot just strip Christianity of its expression through worship and hope to discover pure doctrine or pure anything else—least of all pure Christianity! "The Christian religion is not only a doctrine . . . it is a public action or deed."[2] Christianity grew, developed, and became what it was and is in the context of men and women worshipping the risen Jesus, becoming his body through the overshadowing of the Holy Spirit, and expressing that identity in the liturgy of the Church week in and week out. *Lex orandi lex credendi:* the norm of prayer is the norm of belief. It is no use trying to find the credentials of the Chalcedonian definition of the person of Christ exclusively within the pages of the New Testament. Not unlike a good chef, the full doctrine and practice of the Church always has one ear on the comments and experiences of the customers! It would indeed be a strange doctrine of cooking that always relied exclusively upon the written word of the cookery book for the making of a good omelet. (I suppose there might be gastronomic fundamentalists who turn only to documentary evidence for their basic doctrine, but I suspect they would soon be found almost exclusively in museums and libraries and would no longer be in business in the hotel and restaurant trade!) For wherever, especially today, the Church is really "in business," it is most conspicuously in its worship that we find evidence of its existence.

> The liturgical movement has appeared everywhere clearly bound up with a theological, missionary and spiritual revival. It has been the source of a greater realization by Christians of their responsibility in the world. It has been a revival of the Church herself. . . . It is a return through worship to the Church and through the Church to worship. . . . Christian worship, by its nature, structure and content, is the revelation and realization by the Church of her own real nature. And this nature is the new life in Christ.[3]

Of course, it would be foolish to say that such statements do not also require the checks and balances of other aspects of theology; indeed it would not only be foolish, it could prove disastrous. Today, worship could well be purveyed on the market alongside health cures, personality self-realization, and any other therapy. Such a situation already exists and is big business in the United States. Liturgy and worship for liturgy and worship's sake is perennially in danger of degenerating at best into a mindless and man-centered therapy and at worst into a demonic force. But all this will inevitably happen if worship becomes a separate department in the life of the Church for those who happen to "like that sort of thing." Theology and worship belong together as surely as heart and mind. Each will inform, extend, and correct the other in a single environment. In an ideal Church it will be the bishop who oversees both areas, for he is both principal celebrant in the liturgy and a responsible teacher in the catechetical work of the diocese. The youthful priest Augustine outraged the African church by appearing to unsurp the role of the bishop as preacher when he gave a sermon in the presence of the bishop of Hippo in 393 AD. In the early Church, the bishop was both celebrant and preacher wherever he appeared, thus holding together in his own person a responsibility both for the worship of the Church and also for the teaching ministry. He was in a real sense the "Prime Minister" of word and worship.

This leads us to the second reason for the contemporary alienation of worship and theology—the person of the bishop. In the early Church the bishop was not strictly speaking a hierarchical figure at all, for he had nothing whatever to do with shapes and sizes, but rather with substance. Especially in the Anglican Church, we tend to regard bishops as being kept for "big occasions." Nothing could be further from the image of the bishop in the early Church. He was literally a substantial figure in whom the fullness of the Church in any one area resided. In his person, he reminded the Church both of its unity and also of its plenitude. (It was a later practice of the Medieval Church to place a seventh candle on the altar when the bishop was present to remind the people of the fullness of his office, and it is in fact perhaps still a useful and impressive symbol of the nature of true episcopacy.) This did not mean that the bishop himself was everything in the diocese, from liturgical scholar to principal theologian. But it did most certainly mean that many responsibilities in the Church were delegated through the office of the bishop, and it was clearly seen from the outset that these varying responsibilities were delegated by him and not detached from him. This meant that all the departments of ministry and theology and concern related to each other through the office of the bishop and were preserved in a genuine unity and interrelatedness. The bishop delegated his concerns for worship to the administrator of his cathedral church and he delegated his teaching ministry to his catechists and theologians. But sadly in later years that delegation became a fragmentation to the point where the dean was "in charge of the cathedral" and theologians were the property of the university and of scholarly specialization. So the bishop became little more than a peripatetic traveling managing director, either brought in for big occasions (to match the secular equivalent of mayor, senator, or President) or to write a pastoral charge that, by implication, was not hard-core theology but dealt with soft-edged pastoral concerns largely directed to the clergy. It was surely out of the fragmentation of the bishop's office that the later version of prelacy arose.

There can, in fact, be no lasting or substantial renewal in an episcopal Church without the renewal of the episcopal office. This is one of the most important tasks facing the Church today. The bishop, at least on Sunday and on major feast days, should be in his cathedral church celebrating the liturgy and teaching the Word. That should be the norm. The diocese should run round the bishop and not the bishop round the diocese! Furthermore, his place in confirmation should not consist of a purely mechanical circuit of confirmations, but rather, in his person, he should embody (though necessarily delegate) the responsibilities for the whole of Christian formation and Christian initiation. Thus he is placed where the early bishop belonged and where episcopacy won its spurs, namely, on the cutting edge of the missionary life and risk of the Church. The local parish priests are literally, then, a localization of the bishop's presence and always act as his delegates. All other ministries derive from him and are free to take risks in diversity without becoming schismatic, precisely because the unity is assured and visible in the person of the bishop. It is the bishop who can thus give genuine flexibility to all kinds of local experiments in ministry and mission. In such a revival of the episcopal office there can be no room for a wrong competition—least of all between liturgy and theology—for both flow within the same chemistry, bringing a fullness and richly diverse plenitude to the very heart of the Christian Church, not least to its worship and liturgy.

(I realize, of course, that such a vision of episcopacy will mean much smaller episcopal areas within our Church. The important task, however, will be to multiply genuine episcopacy without multiplying prelacy. We do not need all the trappings of later views of the episcopal office wherever we increase the number of bishops. It is a most urgent and important task facing the Church—not least in America with huge dioceses—and one to which the Church should give its urgent attention as soon as possible.)

The third and final reason for the alienation of worship from all other disciplines and expressions of Christian discipleship is found in the marginalizing of baptism in the Church's liturgy, in the place it holds in the Church's worship-timetable, and in the life of Christian discipleship. It is almost as though the whole Church has conspired over the past two thousand years or more to propagate a doctrine of the "real absence" of baptism from Christian life and worship. Yet in one sense all true Christian worship consists in making explicit the baptismal status of those present. "*Now* are we the sons of God and it does not yet appear what we shall be."[4] For even now we are living out the implications of what it is to be sons and daughters of God our Father and we are already entering upon the promises of the kingdom. Unless that is the background and presupposition of all worship, then there is no way Christian worship can lift the eyes of those who are participating beyond the life of the Church into the environment of the kingdom. For we have seen again and again how contemporary worship lacks a meaningful *anaphora* (a point of "lift-off!") and fails so often to point beyond itself and beyond the life of the Church to the life of the kingdom. For all Christian worship should find its shape and purpose in the shape and purpose of baptism, the bringing of Christ's people through the Red Sea into the land and kingdom of promise. Such a dynamic gives to all Christian worship its purpose and direction. Far from polarizing the Church and the kingdom, it is essential in Christian worship that we "passage" and move over from the Church into the kingdom where Christ's people already belong. "Our conversation is in heaven"[5] is no mere pious platitude. It is the scriptural mandate reflected from the earliest Christian liturgy when Christ's people were commanded to lift up their hearts and to which they rightly responded—by the grace of baptism—"they are already with the Lord."

Yes, "our conversation is in heaven." No study of renewal
in worship can be complete without some reference to language
in worship. For in fact the language of God's people in worship
and their identity are bound up together. The renewal of all the
Churches is increasingly evident throughout the world. Nevertheless, in recent years, there has been another marked shift in the
location and identity of God's people—"a people for his own possession"—in relation to the rest of society. Perhaps nowhere is this
more evident than in English society and its relation to the established Church of England. Since the days of Hooker until very
recently Church and State were regarded as closely related (not
least at a constitutional level), and the Church of England in its
worship represented the spiritual aspirations of a nation. The worship was expressed in language formed during the renaissance of
English literature, in the age of Shakespeare, language at the peak
of its perfection. The beautiful language of the prayer book of the
Church of England in 1662 was part of a cultic package deal, as
surely as Latin, the Roman Catholic Church, and medieval Europe
had also been a package deal. With the Reformation there had been
a cry for worship to be in the vernacular and now, in the twentieth
century, there has occurred another major shift in the location of
the Church in its relation to society. Inevitably this is expressed
in a renewed cry for a new vernacular, but this time it is the language
of the committed minority, increasingly aware of their distinctive
identity as a people for God's own possession, recovering an ever
increasingly "high doctrine" of baptism. There can be no doubt
whatever that all the new liturgies will never again relate so closely
to the whole of culture and society as they did in Christendom
and in sixteenth-century western Europe. Today it is very much
a case of the Church's book for the Church's people in a language
that helps the committed Christian to mean what he says and to
say what he means.

This need not in itself constitute a ghetto mentality. Ghettos
have nothing whatever to do with numbers. A ghetto is an attitude
of mind and such an attitude must be avoided at all costs. Therefore,
all Christians need to develop strongly their vicarious consciousness

for the Christian vocation as a calling to serve God for the whole world, so that we can become God's people in the scriptural sense in which the many are saved by the few and the few are saved by the one. Such a Church should see itself as the leaven, the salt, and the light and must lose all its self-consciousness in a deep worship and love of God and a deep commitment in solidarity with the rest of the world. It is important for the Church to recover this sense of solidarity and vicariousness if it is not to retreat into a ghetto. The Church of God is a representative body of people, doing all that it does on behalf of those who are not its members: that is the "priestly" nature of the Church in relation to the world. St. Paul is adamant: the unbelieving husband is "sanctified" by the believing wife and the unbelieving wife is "sanctified" by the believing husband.[6] From the outset Paul's vision on the road to Damascus had shown him the solidarity of the new race of God in Christ so that he could hear the voice repeatedly accusing him: "Saul, Saul, why are you persecuting *me?*"[7] In order to be such a vicarious and priestly Church, no longer of the world but essentially and always for the world (in fact, if the Church is to be of any earthly use at all), God's people must always have a consciousness that their citizenship and their conversation are both alike in heaven. They will become a "bridge people." Nevertheless, such a consciousness and awareness will involve a break with the culture of the day, which is necessarily secular, and of the age, and nowhere is that break more keenly felt than at the level of language and worship.

The archaic language of the Reformation prayer books belonged increasingly in recent years to a "no-man's-land." You could make it mean as much or as little as you wanted it to mean. To the secularist, it was part of a religious environment he was loath to lose and yet to which he paid less and less attention. But the renewed Christian found that such language inhibited him from expressing his new life in Christ. The break had to come and when it came in the new prayer books throughout the Anglican communion we should not have been surprised at the extent of the furor that accompanied it. After all, in one sense the Christian

Church was robbing society of its religious department. Threaten to pull down temples and you will soon get yourself crucified, and threaten to rob a culture of its religious dimension and you will certainly provoke a plethora of letters to the newspapers at the very least, or petitions even to politicians above the signatures of many who seldom even darken the doors of churches.

But, at last the truth is out! People, by and large, no longer occasionally drift to church on a Sunday morning. If you are a member of the Church you are really a member of the Church and today that will mean belonging week in and week out, with daily Bible reading and studies of the Scriptures, perhaps tithing, and possibly regularly attending a prayer group, with a refresher course, and an annual retreat thrown in for good measure. If, on the other hand, you are not a member of the Church, then apart from a wistful desire for a return of the old prayer book (or the Latin Mass as the case may be) on occasions of national celebration, you will feel that the Church is out of touch, though—strangely enough—not quite for the same reasons your grandparents thought that the Church was out of touch. In those days they used to say that the Church was out of touch because it appeared somewhat "holier than thou," but today the complaint is more likely to be that we are not holy enough: too many guitars and not enough thee's and thou's!

All this is inevitable and by no means wholly undesirable, providing that our missionary zeal grows and burns ever more brightly. The opportunity for instruction, learning groups, catechesis, and the Christian apologetic must claim a new priority in the life of the Church. Increasingly, we must present an apologetic that is able to talk about the truth and to commend itself at the level of truth to readers of *Time* magazine or *The New York Times*. For too long the Christian church has pursued its missionary zeal as if it had a clubby mentality and wanted to encourage people to come to church and join a club. The result is so often that most ugly and self-conscious feature of the Church—a body of people who are committed but not converted.

All the time—and at the same time—Christian worship and

intercession must be heavily clad with the vision of the Church as representative of humanity: a true priesthood of *all* believers (which is not the same thing as the priesthood of each believer); a people committed to the worship of God in the world and on behalf of the world, matching the priesthood of the one who died for the world, was raised and glorified and ever lives now to make intercession for all mankind. For in true worship we are doing the work of God for the world. We are uniting with that one great offering of Christ, which was essentially for the whole universe. That vision, and nothing less than that vision, will prevent a renewed and committed Church from turning its back upon the world and retreating into a ghetto of its own concerns.

So worship must not be just "down to earth," otherwise it will be exclusive, worship for those bits of the earth that like that sort of thing. Only worship that raises our prayers and praises and unites them with the prayer of Christ and all his saints in heaven will necessarily be representative. When the Levitical priest entered the holy of holies in the Old Testament he wore an ephod and on the ephod over his heart were the emblems of the twelve tribes of Israel whom he represented. The particularity of the vocation of the tribe of Levi was not an exclusive vocation but a representative vocation. That is always true of all vocations within the whole Body. They are distinctive and different, but never privileged or exclusive. So many discussions about the priesthood have assumed that a distinctive doctrine of the vocation to the priestly life automatically assumes that it is an exclusive and excluding vocation. Nothing could be more contrary to the biblical view of vocation. In the vocation of the tribe of Levi, we see the paradox of the proper exclusiveness of Christians, the Church, and its worship. We must wear the concerns of the world on our hearts, but it is no good to be all dressed up with nowhere to go! These hearts, heavy with the concerns of the world and our community, must also be "raised" if they are really to help that community and vicariously bring the community into the presence of God in Christ through intercession. That is what the word intercession literally means. To intercede is to go into the presence of a person on behalf of another. If we are before God in Christ, we are in his Body together with all his holy people—visible and invisible, known and unknown. Then we are truly where we belong as a Church and we are truly both serving the world and serving God. The transfigured Christ was with holy Moses and holy Elias. The risen Christ is with his saints, and his saints are with him, for they are also the Body of Christ and in Christ we are one with them. All our worship must bring us into the kingdom and raise us into the fellowship of the saints, together with "angels and archangels and with all the company of heaven." Only such heavenly worship is any earthly use at all. So, whether it is at the bedside of an old lady who is dying or at the glorious worship of a huge congregation in a vast basilica; whether it is with two or three huddled together in prison on the eve of their execution, singing hymns at midnight like Paul and Silas, or locked up in the basilica like Ambrose with his congregation in Milan; whether in a hospital ward or in a trench before battle; there is no corner of earth and no gathering too insignificant that cannot be raised beyond itself in Christ into the presence of the Father with all the saints, "enkingdomed," transfigured, and glorified. So we all can become even now (for those with eyes to see) what we were intended to be from eternity and will be in Christ throughout all ages and world without end. "In our religion, and in all the worship which is the expression of our religion, we look out towards eternity; and bit by bit, in various ways and degrees, we discover in ourselves a certain capacity for eternity."[8]

10

Now and Forever

IF WORSHIP OPENS US TO "a certain capacity for eternity" (as we saw at the conclusion of the last chapter), we must avoid any reduction within worship that might imprison us within what is merely contemporary. Renewal has very little whatever to do with modernity, vogue, or fashion. On the contrary, worship, as we have seen in an earlier chapter, takes us down "memory lane," recalling previous experiences that have touched and moved us. Associated with those experiences have been words, places, times, tunes—even smells—so that there is an inevitable element of conservatism in our attitudes to worship. It is true of course that these associations are so powerful that we are always in danger of mistaking the means of worship with the true object of our worship. If we are not careful, the church building (including its furniture and fittings) where we worshipped as children, where we were married, where we shed tears in bereavement, may not just be the environment in which we worship, but can become the actual object of our worship. That is just plain, old-fashioned idolatry, and all worshippers need to know the danger of that kind of idolatry. It is never very far below the surface in many vestry meetings, when liturgy and worship are being discussed!

The clergy and those responsible for fashioning and leading worship need to know a second and perhaps more important principle. Worship is never (on earth) so clean, disinfected, and "spiritual"

that it has no *location* and no geography. Worship is rooted in the
senses, as surely as love is related to the body. Surgery in either
category is likely to prove equally traumatic! Furthermore, because
both worship and love belong to a complex of associations, we
cannot approach either of them in a totally clean, logical, or straightforward way. Most of the *logical* arguments about why one way
of doing the service is better than another fall on deaf ears. Logic
is only one of many motivations in worship, and it is probably the
least powerful.

That is why the advent of a new Prayer Book in the national
Church, or a "new service" in the local church can always be guaran-
teed to open a whole can of worms. We are tampering with something that goes deeply into the recesses of people's experience,
and everyone (including the clergy) will be approaching this subject
with all kinds of hidden agendas. You play and interfere with worship at your peril. Words, phrases, even the tunes of hymns, are
loaded and heavy with deep associations.

Of course this does not mean that there can never be changes
of any kind in liturgy and worship. Worship is a living response
to what is changeless, and worship will always be seeking new ways
of expression. So perhaps we need a principle to guide us through
this dense and complicated territory, mined as it is with all kinds
of unexpected and unpredictable explosives.

The principle is what I have come to call *the principle of gradation*.
There are two points in this principle we need to affirm in all
liturgical change. The first point is that continuity must be more
evident than discontinuity. The second point is that in all new
expressions of worship (especially in music), roughly ninety percent
of what is new will prove to be unsubstantial and not lasting
and only ten percent will "abide" and become part of the tradition.
Let us look at these two points within the principle of gradation
and see how they will apply in practice.

Continuity and discontinuity are written into life at its most
basic level, even into our biological evolution. We evolve by both
continuity and discontinuity. There is much about everyday life
that is everyday. We get our bearings from the familiar, from things

we come to rely upon—from the alarm going off in the morning to the sun setting in the west in the evening. Yet within those predetermined experiences, we choose to make breaks with previous patterns, to strike out into new and different ways. Always there is both continuity and discontinuity, otherwise we simply would not know who we are or where we are. Our identity and our direction are derived from our past, and with much of it we need to be able to take it for granted.

In worship this factor is even more powerfully at work. Tradition is not a dusty word, imprisoning us in the past. It is the dynamic of all life. "I hand on to you that which I first received."[1] Tradition does not mean getting stuck in the past. Tradition is not sticking to the facts; it is allowing the facts to stick to us! The nearest analogy is that of the frequent flyer with many American airlines. The frequent flyer has little stickers. He sticks them to the ticket every time he travels. He sticks his past mileage on his present ticket and eventually it opens up for him a wonderful future of free flight! So with tradition. The past sticks to the present giving it a new potential and enriching it so that we can go with confidence into God's future for us. If, however, we cut off our past, we rob the present of its potential. It is only those who have a strong tradition who can afford (literally) to be least conservative. The radical is someone who is so secure at the center that he can afford to go to the edges of experiment.

It was an unfortunate oversimplification that led the Episcopal Church in America to *replace* the old Prayer Book with the new. In the Church of England the law of the land prevented the Church from that form of discontinuity. Legally there is only one prayer book to this day in the Church of England, and that is the Book of Common Prayer of 1662. The so-called "new prayer book" is not able to replace *the* Prayer Book of 1662 without an Act of Parliament. So the "new Book" is in fact called The Alternative Service Book 1980—and that is precisely what it is. In other words, the old and the new will continue to run alongside and overlap with each other. That, frankly, is the most responsible way of changing worship. (Admittedly, the Church of England should claim no virtue from this situation. It is an accident of law and history, but it has probably prevented the English Church from cutting off its tail and imposing the new book by forsaking or abolishing the old.)

Yet change there must be—even in language. We know that no prayer book could equal the aesthetic beauty of the English language of the Book of 1662. It so happened that when Cranmer was putting the medieval Latin services into English, he was doing it when the English language was entering its renaissance—its Shakespearian excellence. Technically, no contemporary language will be able to equal that of the sixteenth century because that period marked the high-water mark of the language's renaissance.

Nevertheless, as a Reformation church, the Anglican Church is committed to the vernacular; it is a betrayal of that principle if we refuse to conduct worship in the vernacular. The time is long overdue for language revision, while recognizing that "words, even agreed words, are only the beginning of worship. Those who use them do well to recognize their transience and imperfection; to treat them as a ladder, not a goal."[2] So, as the principle of gradation urges, we should not cut off our tail, lose all continuity with the past, and start with clean, disinfected language and new words for their own sake. There must be continuity and overlap, especially in those very areas where prayer and worship have become part of the common subconscious religious experience of a whole generation. The most obvious example of this is the Lord's Prayer, which thankfully occurs in parallel translations in the 1979 Prayer Book. A sensitive pastor would surely never arrive at the bedside of a dying occasional churchgoer and recite the Lord's Prayer in its modern form. It would simply fail to resonate with anything in the person's past experience of God and would therefore be less powerful to bring comfort, strength, and reassurance. Some "new Christians" come to mind, however, whose prayer reflex-action would automatically lead them off in the new translation of familiar prayers and responses without a second thought. Generations overlap, and the Church has to learn to live with this overlapping even in an untidy way for several decades to come.

For (and this is the second point in the principle of gradation) we need to realize that much of what is new will not wear well. It will simply be found (on experience and with frequent use) to be lightweight. This is especially true with so much in worship. After all it is true generally for the whole art of music throughout history. There were all kinds of composers in the eighteenth century, many of them remarkably popular in their own day, but it is the music of the Mozarts and Beethovens (probably less than ten percent of the total output of the age) that has lasted. It is foolish and irresponsible to choose new hymns for all the hymns of a service. It is encouraging to see that the choice of hymns for the new Church Hymnal for the Episcopal Church is wisely based on the principle of gradation.

> As the church itself is continually being made new, so the music of the Church has reflected the life of its many generations. The Hymnal has been and will be an essential part of the record of this life and growth. It should retain classic texts and music which have been honored by history and are staples for singing congregations. At the same time it should present a prophetic vision that will speak to the Church of the future as well as the Church of today.[3]

Three cheers! The key phrase in that statement of intention is the phrase "at the same time." Like the architecture of a great cathedral, the best features of different periods can live happily alongside and in juxtaposition. Don't put all your eggs in one basket—be it old or new—and realize that not all the eggs will prove to be equally good. Hopefully most musical settings to the Eucharist will not survive the decade! They don't deserve to. Yet possibly, and hopefully, one in ten will, and we shall only discover that one by use and through experience and experiment. The new hymnal has a solid staple diet of known hymns that have become the "folk songs" of God's people. It also includes a good selection of new hymns and spiritual songs. It is to be commended on the balance and content: it has got them right. Let this approach be our approach to all liturgical change and modernization, and then we shall avoid some of the heartbreaks of 1976 and subsequently.

For even in the resurrection there will not be total discontinuity. The risen Christ was "new" yet still just recognizable, and Paul does not present his doctrine of the resurrection life as though it is or will be a total break with what we have come to know and to be at home with in this world.

> In this present frame we sigh with deep longing for the heavenly house, for we do not want to face utter nakedness when death destroys our present dwelling—these bodies of ours. So long as we are clothed in this temporary dwelling we have a powerful longing, not because we want just to get rid of these "clothes" but because we want to know the full cover of the permanent home that will be ours. We want our transitory life to be absorbed into the life that is eternal.[4]

So with our worship. It is not only powerful through past associations, but it also yearns and reaches forward to the perfect worship of heaven with all the saints. It is not just a familiar tune we have known and with which we have many associations (though it is that at the very least). It is also at the same time the "echo of a tune we have not yet heard." And somewhere in all this is a single seamless garment: and it is a deep offense to tear it and divide it into past, present, and future, old, or new.

For all our worship on earth is to prepare us for the life and worship of heaven—where life will be worship, and where to worship will be a whole way of life, eternal life. God's people in their worship have "caught on" to this truth and in turn are "caught up" by their worship into the life and worship of the saints in heaven, where change is now part of changelessness and where the new is now enveloped by eternity. That is the point of churchgoing, and it is a point the laity in the pews, the organist at the console, the choir at their anthem books, the acolytes with their torches, the reader at the lectern, the preacher in the pulpit, and the priest at the altar should never forget. They do so at their peril—an eternal peril. For when worship misses the point it ceases to be anything worthy of our attention. Instead of being an investment in eternity, it becomes simply a waste of time. Yet when time is used for worship, it becomes eternal ("the time simply flew by")—as every lover and worshipper knows from experience. Or perhaps it just stood still. So about all our worship there must always be something of this "other" and in all changes (necessary and important though they are in this world) we must never lose what is changeless, because although it can be discovered in time (where change is inevitable), it can only be known and made our own in eternity. "Then we shall be still and see, we shall see and we shall love, we shall love and we shall praise. Behold what will be, in the end, without end! For what is our end but to reach that kingdom which has no end."[5]

Notes

CHAPTER ONE: WORSHIP AND THE HUMAN CONDITION

1. Peter Shaffer, *Equus*, act 2 (Avon, 1977).
2. P. Gerhardt, "The duteous day now closeth," *English Hymnal* (1940), Hymn 181.
3. C. Wesley, "Love divine, all loves excelling," *English Hymnal* (1940), Hymn 479.
4. Colin Dunlop, *Anglican Public Worship* (SCM Press, 1953), 14.
5. Isa. 33:9-20.
6. Exod. 7:16 and 8:1.
7. John 4:24.
8. Prayer Book Collect, Trinity VI, Medieval version.
9. Gal. 5:1.
10. Acts 2:15.
11. William Temple, *Christian Faith and Life* (Morehouse, 1982).
12. Rev. 7:9-11.
13. Shakespeare, *Troilus and Cressida*, act 1, sc. 3, line 109.
14. A.N. Whitehead, *Science and the Modern World* (Free Press, 1967).

CHAPTER TWO: THE NATURE AND CHARACTERISTICS
OF CHRISTIAN WORSHIP

1. 1 John 4:19.
2. Mark 1:11 and 9:7.

3. Eph. 5:2.
4. 1 Kgs. 18:20-40.
5. William Temple, *The Preacher's Theme Today* (SPCK), 20.
6. Isa. 44:9-12; 46:5-7.
7. C.S. Lewis, "The Weight of Glory" in *They Asked for a Paper* (Macmillan, 1980).
8. 1 Kgs. 18:21.
9. Gen. 28:10-22.
10. Lev. 19:2.
11. 1 Sam. 15:22-23.
12. Amos 5:21-24.
13. Isa. 1:12-17.
14. Ecclus. 34:19.
15. Ecclus. 35:6.
16. Ps. 40 (Coverdale Translation).
17. Col. 1:24.
18. Ps. 136.
19. Henry Scott-Holland, *A Bundle of Memories* (Wells, Gardner & Darton, 1915), 61.
20. George Herbert, "King of glory, King of peace," *English Hymnal* 424, v.3.
21. Phil. 3:20.

CHAPTER THREE: WORSHIP AND THE CHURCH TODAY

1. W.H. Vanstone, *The Risk of Love* (Oxford University Press, 1978).
2. Rom. 12:1.
3. William Temple, *The Hope of New World* (Ayer Co., 1940).
4. William Temple, *The Church and Its Teaching Today* (Macmillan), 15.
5. 1 Clement 40:41.
6. Acts 20:28; 1 Pet. 5:3.
7. Eph. 4:3.
8. M. de Unamuno, *The Tragic Sense of Life* (Dover, 1921).
9. Frère Roger Schultz, *Festival* (SPCK, 1971), 48f.
10. Colin Dunlop, *Anglican Public Worship* (SCM Press, 1953), 51f.

CHAPTER FOUR: UNITY AND FLEXIBILITY IN WORSHIP

1. Eccles. 4:12.
2. 1 Cor. 15:46.

CHAPTER FIVE: MUSIC AND WORSHIP

1. C. Henry Phillips, *The Singing Church* (Faber & Faber Ltd, 1945), 238.
2. Winifred Douglas, *Church Music in History and Practice* (New York: Charles Scribner's Sons, 1940), 9f.
3. Acts 16:25.
4. Douglas, *Church Music in History and Practice*, 28f.
5. *Psalm Praise*, (London: Falcon, 1973).
6. Betty Pulkingham and Jeanne Harper, *Sound of Living Waters* (Eerdmans, 1974).
7. Phillips, *The Singing Church*, 238.
8. Douglas, *Church Music in History and Practice*, 8.

CHAPTER SIX: SIGNS, SYMBOLS, AND CEREMONIES

1. Isa. 29:18-19; 35:5-6; 61:1.
2. Luke 7:18-23.
3. Thomas Carlyle, *Sartor Resartus* (Arden Library, 1981).
4. Christopher Bryant, *The River Within* (Upper Room, 1983).
5. Ezek. 3:1-3; Jer. 18.
6. *New American Prayer Book*, 306.
7. Ezek. 47.
8. Clifford Howell, "The Communion Rite—The Deterioration of the Signs," *Liturgy* 2, no. (St. Paul Publications), 237.
9. Matt. 5:16.
10. Alexander Schmemann, (St. Vladimir's, 1973).
11. John Austin Baker, *The Whole Family of God* (Mowbray, 1981), 172f.
12. Wisdom 18:14-15.
13. William Cowper, "Jesus, where'er thy people meet," *English Hymnal* 422, v.4.

CHAPTER SEVEN: RECEIVING THE WORD OF GOD

1. Luke 24:13-35.
2. Heb. 4:12-13.
3. Isa. 55:11.
4. 1 Thess. 2:13.
5. John 14:26; 16:15.
6. Matt. 10:32.
7. Robert E. Terwilliger, *Receiving the Word of God* (New York: Morehouse-Barlow & Co, 1960), 140.
8. Ezek. 3:1.
9. Collect for second Sunday in Advent, *Book of Common Prayer* (Episcopal).
10. Luke 24:46-48.
11. St. Augustine, Sermon 17:1.
12. St. Augustine, "De Doctrina Christiana," Book 4, 42:6.
13. D. Coggan, *Stewards of Grace* (Hodder & Stoughton, 1958), 18.
14. St. Augustine, Sermon 133:1.
15. St. Augustine, Sermon (Guelfergitanus), 19:2.
16. Paul Simon, "Sounds of Silence" (Eclectic Music Co., 1965).
17. John R.W. Stott, *Between Two Worlds* (Eerdman, 1982).
18. St. Augustine, "Sermons on St. John's gospel," 19:9 and 1:133.
19. St. Augustine, "De catechizandis rudibus," 13:19; 209.
20. St. Augustine, "Enarrationes in Psalmos," Ps. 36, 3:6.
21. Terwilliger, *Receiving the Word of God*, 135.
22. St. Augustine, "De Doctrina Christiana," Book 4, 12:27; 136.
23. Terwilliger, *Receiving the Word of God*, 122.
24. Ibid., 124.
25. Ibid., 131.
26. E.C. Dargan, *A History of Preaching*, Vol. 1, AD 70–1572 (B. Franklin, 1965).
27. D. Martyn Lloyd-Jones, *Preaching and Preachers* (Zandervan, 1972).
28. Decree on the Ministry and Life of Priests, Second Vatican Council.

CHAPTER EIGHT: WORSHIP, SERVICE, AND LIFE
1. William Temple, *Citizen and Churchman* (Eyre & Spottiswood), 101.
2. Eph. 4:9-10.
3. Acts 10:9-16.
4. John 6:12.
5. Aldous Huxley, *The Doors of Perception* (Penguin Books in association with Chatto & Windus, 1959), 35.
6. William Temple, *Christian Faith and Life* (SCM Press), 18.
7. Ibid.
8. Temple, *Citizen and Churchman*, 101.
9. Matt. 25:40.
10. 1 Cor. 11:29.
11. St. John Chrysostom, Homily 50:3-4.
12. Temple, *Christian Faith and Life* (SCM Press), 19.
13. Acts 3:8-10.
14. Luke 18:43.
15. Luke 11:39.
16. John 2:7.
17. Luke 6:38.
18. Matt. 5:41.
19. Matt. 5:40.
20. 2 Sam. 24:24.
21. Isaac Watts, "When I survey the Wondrous Cross" *English Hymnal* (1940), Hymn 337.
22. Luke 17:10.

CHAPTER NINE: "WITH ANGELS AND ARCHANGELS AND WITH ALL THE COMPANY OF HEAVEN"

1. Alexander Schmemann, *Introduction to Liturgical Theology* (Vladimirs, 1966).
2. Louis Bouyer, *Le Mystere Paschal* (Les editions du cerf, Paris, 1947), 9.
3. Schmemann, *Introduction to Liturgical Theology*, 12, 23.
4. 1 John 3:2.
5. Phil. 3:20.
6. 1 Cor. 7:14.

7. Acts 9:1-9.
8. Evelyn Underhill, *The Mystery of Sacrifice* (Longmans Green & Co Ltd, 1959), Introduction.

CHAPTER 10: NOW AND FOREVER

1. 1 Cor. 15:3.
2. Preface to *The Alternative Service Book* (London: Hodder and Stoughton, 1980).
3. Forward to New Church Hymnal.
4. 2 Cor. 5:2ff.
5. St. Augustine, Conclusion to *The City of God*.

64962